AF606048

THE CRISIS-WOMAN

Body Politics and the Modern Woman in Fascist Italy

NATASHA V. CHANG

The Crisis-Woman

Body Politics and the Modern Woman in Fascist Italy

UNIVERSITY OF TORONTO PRESS
Toronto Buffalo London

Toronto Buffalo London
www.utppublishing.com

ISBN 978-1-4426-4967-5

Toronto Italian Studies

Library and Archives Canada Cataloguing in Publication

Chang, Natasha V., 1971–, author
The crisis-woman : body politics and the modern woman in fascist Italy / Natasha V. Chang.

(Toronto Italian studies)
Includes bibliographical references and index.
ISBN 978-1-4426-4967-5 (bound)

1. Fascism and women – Italy – History – 20th century. 2. Women in popular culture – Italy – History – 20th century. 3. Women – Italy – Social conditions – 20th century. 4. Italy – Social conditions – 1918–1945. 5. Fascism – Italy – History – 20th century. I. Title. II. Series: Toronto Italian studies

HQ1236.5.I8C43 2014 305.42094509'043 C2014-906558-2

This book has been published with the assistance of Middlebury College.
University of Toronto Press acknowledges the financial assistance to its publishing program of the Canada Council for the Arts and the Ontario Arts Council, an Ontario government agency.

Canada Council for the Arts Conseil des Arts du Canada

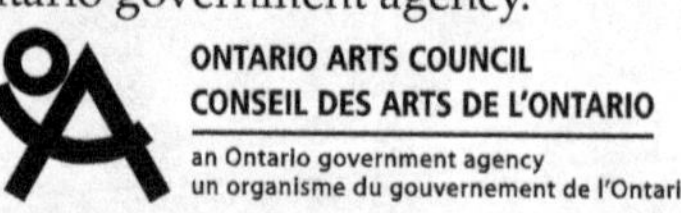

University of Toronto Press acknowledges the financial support of the Government of Canada through the Canada Book Fund for its publishing activities.

Contents

Illustrations

Acknowledgments

I have benefited from a wonderful community of support, both professional and personal, during the writing of this book. For the time spent reading all or parts of this manuscript – from its incipient to its final form – I wish to thank several of my friends and colleagues: Gina Herrmann, Elvira Vilches, Luca Caminati, Paula Schwartz, Yumna Siddiqi, and Leif Sorensen. Their camaraderie helped me push through the most difficult moments of writing, and their rigorous commentary helped me both expand and refine my ideas. I am grateful also to Frank Snowden and the participants of the NEH seminar "Italian Fascism: History and Interpretations" for the informative and spirited discussions that led me to explore areas beyond my expertise and helped me find the confidence to let go of the last vestiges of my doctoral dissertation in order to create an entirely new work. I would also like to express warm thanks to John Tallmadge for his tireless encouragement and for his help in organizing the project in its early stages. A special thanks to Alessandro Visani, whose friendship, advice, and assistance with matters great and small has been invaluable. Finally, I wish to express my deep thanks to the two anonymous readers from the University of Toronto Press whose insightful commentary and criticism helped me see my work more clearly, consider several key issues from a fresh perspective, and gave me the fortitude to improve the manuscript when I felt I didn't have it in me to do more.

My research was generously funded in part by the Middlebury College Faculty Professional Development Fund and a Starr Winter Term Faculty Development Grant. The logistical and knowledgeable support of the staff of the Biblioteca Nazionale Centrale of Florence, the Biblioteca Nazionale Braidense in Milan, the Biblioteca Nazionale

Centrale in Rome, the Bibliothèque Nationale in Paris, and the Library of Congress in Washington, DC, were all crucial. Thanks also to Rachel Manning in the Middlebury College Interlibrary Loan Department for her assistance in obtaining key texts from Italy as well as to Cynthia Slater in Library and Information Services for her help in formatting the manuscript. It has been a privilege and a great pleasure to work with my editor Siobhan McMenemy as well as the late Ron Schoeffel, both of whom have been reassuring and expert guides through the publishing process.

I am deeply grateful for the continuous support and encouragement of my parents, Nada and Sai Chang, in all my endeavours. My uncle and aunt, Slavko Rehnicer and Antonella Sordi, have provided me and my family with generous hospitality and conviviality during our frequent stays in Italy. I owe a special debt to Christine Hoar, teacher and friend, who has given me the gift of a life-long practice that kept me healthy in body and mind as I worked on this project. Finally, and above all, my greatest debt is to my dearest friend and life partner Timothy Billings, who has seen me through every step of writing this manuscript, who has read carefully and caringly every word that follows, who believed in my ability to complete this work in the face of all contrary evidence, and who lovingly sustains me in my day-to-day life. This book is dedicated to Timothy and our daughter Viviana.

THE CRISIS-WOMAN

Body Politics and the Modern Woman in Fascist Italy

Introduction
Who Is the Crisis-Woman?

Consider the following cartoon printed in a satirical newspaper in Italy approximately a decade after the establishment of the fascist regime: a man relaxes in an easy chair at home and is interrupted by a maid announcing a caller (Figure 1). "Who wants me, a gentleman?" he asks. "No," the maid replies. "A lady?" he inquires again. "No," she replies once more. "Well, then, who is it?" he insists. "It's a crisis-woman," the maid answers smugly.[1] Readers unfamiliar with Italian fascist culture might well wonder who – or what – a crisis-woman is, and in doing so they would inadvertently pinpoint the crux of the joke, which is the unintelligibility of the figure. In order to unpack this joke, one must first know that the crisis-woman, or *donna-crisi,* was in the fascist imagination a dangerous type of well-to-do modern woman with an extremely thin and consequently sterile body that purportedly confirmed her cosmopolitan, non-domestic, non-maternal, and non-fascist interests. One assumes that the maid has opened the door to a caller who in some way fits this physical description, and cleverly reports back to the master of the house with a quip. The key to the humour of the cartoon lies in the maid's disdainful reference to the crisis-woman as neither a gentleman nor a lady – that is, neither male nor female but an incomprehensible third sex.[2] In fascist Italy, the thinness and sterility of the crisis-woman were viewed as a deviant masculinization of the naturally curvaceous and fertile female body. This deviance placed the *donna-crisi* outside the realm of cultural intelligibility – and arguably, at the time, outside the realm of biological intelligibility – making her an object of ridicule suitable for a satirical cartoon. I begin with this domestic scene, depicted by the noted Neapolitan illustrator Ugo de Vargas and published in the biweekly comic and satirical newspaper *Marc'Aurelio,* because it tells us

Donna Crisi

— Chi mi desidera, un signore?
— No.
— Una signora?
— No.
— Insomma chi è?
— E' una donna crisi.

(Disegno di De Vargas)

Figure 1. The cartoon "Donna Crisi" published in *Marc'Aurelio* (1933). The captions read: "Who wants me, a gentleman?" "No." "A lady?" "No." "Well then, who is it?" "It's a crisis-woman." (By permission of the Ministero dei beni e delle attività culturali e del turismo della Repubblica Italiana/Biblioteca Nazionale Centrale di Firenze. Reproduction prohibited.)

much about the regime's understanding of and attitudes towards modern women. De Vargas's work illustrates in miniature a larger cultural phenomenon characteristic of fascist Italy that I explore throughout this book, namely the manner in which social, cultural, and political anxieties about evolving gender roles often centred on phantasmatic and stereotyped images of the modern woman – and more specifically on images of the body of the modern woman. In addition, De Vargas's work points to the crucial rhetorical and ideological role that the notion of crisis played in such images.

The central figure of this book is a uniquely Italian representation of the modern woman: the negative figure of fascist propaganda called the *donna-crisi*. The *donna-crisi* possessed many of the typical characteristics of the modern woman – she was fashionable, worldly, emancipated, and a challenge to traditional gender norms – but unlike many other non-fascist representations of the modern woman, she was invariably represented in negative terms. Produced and disseminated by the regime, the crisis-woman was intended to be an abject caricature of the modern woman that particularly emphasized and ridiculed her propensity to follow the trend of thinning down that became popular in the 1920s and endured well beyond those years. I provide a detailed description of my object of study below, but suffice it here to say that in the early 1930s fascist propaganda argued that the modern woman was more often than not a "crisis-woman" who threatened Italy's health with her slender body. In the opinion of fascist ideologues, thinness lead to sterility – a dangerous and particularly modern condition that if left unaddressed would contribute to a rapidly declining birth rate and result in the weakening and eventual death of the nation. De Vargas's cartoon is a good example of satire that is in line with the regime's political and ideological goals insofar as it depicts fascism's fantasized solution to the problematic appeal of the thin modern woman: she is literally erased from the picture as if she were too terrible for the reader to lay eyes upon. Instead, the only image of femininity that the reader sees – the reader, who not inconsequently is mirrored by the man of the house also holding a copy of "Marc'Aurelio" – is the voluptuous maid whose round hips and breasts are accentuated by her cocked stance and set off by the curtain behind her. In this typical fascist fantasy, the problematic, emancipated, thin modern woman is replaced by the accommodating, curvaceous, and self-satisfied domestic servant.

Despite the obvious scholarly appeal of a transgressive woman who was unabashedly cosmopolitan and more interested in the latest fashions than in the duties of motherhood, the *donna-crisi* has remained on the margins of study. In her comprehensive book *How Fascism Ruled Women*, for example, historian Victoria de Grazia writes: "Fascist propaganda manufactured two female images. One was the *donna-crisi*: she was cosmopolitan, urbane, skinny, hysterical, decadent, and sterile. The other was the *donna-madre*: she was national, rural, floridly robust, tranquil, and prolific."[3] Although de Grazia comments decisively on the crisis-woman both here and elsewhere, it is always within the context of a larger argument, and her discussions of the figure are necessarily brief.[4] References to the *donna-crisi* can be found throughout scholarship on women in fascist Italy: in the work of Natalia Aspesi, Grazietta Chiesa Butazzi, Rossana De Longis, Helga Dittrich-Johansen, Stephen Gundle, Elisabetta Mondello, Robin Pickering-Iazzi, and others.[5] Each of these scholars refers to the crisis-woman, and yet none pursues the figure in detail, and some even erroneously perceive her as a widespread phenomenon of the period. In sum, although the crisis-woman has her place in the broader Italian cultural imagination, it is not a central one, and her significance has been typically understood in rather simplistic terms.

This book brings the crisis-woman to centre stage in order to historicize and contextualize more precisely a figure that has often been mistaken as a common phenomenon of the fascist period. In the chapters that follow I present a rich series of previously unexamined primary sources that allow me to detail the historical and physical contours of this intriguing figure as never before. In doing so, I aim to contribute to a growing body of scholarship that shows how representations of women in the fascist period extended beyond the well-known stereotype of the prolific mother and self-sacrificing housewife to include figures that were unexpectedly heterogeneous and often unabashedly modern. The crisis-woman is an image that merits special consideration, however, because she is arguably the most prominent negative propaganda figure of femininity produced and disseminated by the regime. For a brief period this key figure became the flashpoint for a wide range of anxieties that included everything from the changing social roles of urban women to the slippage of stable racial boundaries between the Italian nation and its colonies. This book not only gives scholars a more complete picture of the figure of the *donna-crisi*, but also provides a more complex picture of the manner in which the regime's gendered body politics operated, and ultimately serves as an important case study for the way fascist ideology strategically deployed the notion of crisis.

With its play on the crisis of meaning provoked by the presence (or, to be more precise, absence) of the desexed *donna-crisi,* de Vargas's cartoon perfectly illustrates the two central and recurring themes of this book – the construction of crisis and the construction of the female body – both of which warrant some comment here. For the fascist regime, the body was a crucial instrument of control and shaping the physical body was a profoundly political act, even if at the level of the individual it concerned seemingly frivolous choices such as which fashion trends to follow and which to reject. Many scholars have observed that the regime viewed the Italian nation as a body to be protected and defended, and that it operated on the premise that the process of building a cohesive nation from disparate groups of people began by building the bodies of individuals – in particular, the bodies of women. David Horn emphasizes this last point when he argues in *Social Bodies* that "the female body was seen as the locus of greater dangers and potentials" during the fascist period, and that "women's everyday practices were privileged sites of surveillance and intervention" for the regime."[6] But studies of the female body under the regime have primarily concentrated on idealized types such as the prolific *donna-madre,* who is described very well by Victoria de Grazia, or the healthy, athletic "fascist new woman," who is the subject of Gigliola Gori's book *Italian Fascism and the Female Body.* Similarly, scholarship on the male body under the regime has focused almost exclusively on hegemonic articulations such as the futurist machine-body or the body of Mussolini. The present study takes a different approach insofar as I examine an *abject* female body in order to map out an alternative genealogy of femininity in this period. My approach to the material presented is also distinct insofar as I concentrate on the processes by which power is discursively inscribed upon the female body rather than on the question of consensus and resistance to fascist models of female corporeality, as does most previous scholarship. My aim in both of these choices is to complicate the models of power and subjectivity that have so far been proposed, and to explore how the modern woman – like the "Jew" or "African" in the fascist imagination – becomes at times an objectification of, and repository for, negativity. Throughout this book I show how the abject body of the *donna-crisi* is an important ideological construct that helped produce a set of social and bodily norms that not only conformed to but also produced fascist models of female subjectivity, and I ultimately argue that the crisis-woman tells us as much about the operations of fascist ideology as it does about ideas of the modern female body that existed under the regime.

The writings of several theorists who discuss the body in relation to political power and ideology serve as the infrastructure that sustains the core arguments of this book. Especially relevant is Michel Foucault's notion of "biopower," a political technology of power that involves the "disciplinary surveillance" of the body, both on the part of the individual and on the part of institutions such as the state; it ultimately produces a "docile" body or one that willingly conforms to the strategies and desires of those in authority.[7] Following a Foucauldian line of thought, I show in the first three chapters of this book that to trace the contours of the body of the *donna-crisi* is to trace the relation between discourse, forms of knowledge, political power, and the ideological process of self-constitution. Also central to this book is Judith Butler's formulation of "bodies that matter" versus those that are abject and lie outside the domain of cultural intelligibility. Butler's formulation of the abject – which puts the psychoanalytic work of Julia Kristeva into dialogue with political theorists like Ernesto Laclau and Chantal Mouffe – and her theorization of the body in general ground my recurrent argument that the contours of the undesirable body of the *donna-crisi* are intimately related to the contours of positive, wholesome models of fascist femininity like the *donna-madre*.[8] Finally, what might be called the post-Marxist trajectory outlined from Foucault to Butler takes me naturally to Slavoj Zizek's formulation of ideological fantasy for my concluding discussion of the crisis-woman as a figure crucial to fascist ideology.

Although I make ample use of historical scholarship throughout this study in order to contextualize the new primary sources I present, my methodology as a literary scholar is to consider how texts accrue symbolic value through signifying processes that exceed literal and even connotative domains. Thus, in this book I combine historical investigation with literary strategies of reading. As the chapters unfold, two interrelated readings of the figure of the crisis-woman will emerge, the first historical and symptomatic, and the second rhetorical and ideological. First, I read the *donna-crisi* as a figure that is symptomatic of a variety of historical shifts, as well as of fascism's response to them. I show in chapter 1, for example, how the sterility and distastefully masculine attributes of the crisis-woman reveal a displaced fear of changing gender roles that accompanied the modernization so needed and desired by the regime. Similarly, in chapter 2 I demonstrate that the depiction of the *donna-crisi* as a skeletal creature points to political anxieties about the waning demographic power of the nation. I also argue in chapter 4, however, that the *donna-crisi* must be understood as a symbolically overdetermined figure that is integral to fascist ideology. My overall claim is that the *donna-crisi* does not simply describe or reflect crisis as a simple index of social, economic, and historical realities, but rather that the figure of the *donna-crisi* must be examined for the structural, performative, and tautological role she plays in fascist ideology.

On a larger scale, then, this book is a reflection on the political and ideological effects of the term "crisis" during the fascist period in Italy. While most scholars point to crisis as a factor that generated fascism, this study examines how and to what ends fascism *itself* generated the idea of crisis. I emphasize that the regime strategically manufactured and deployed the notion of crisis in order to realize its goals – a tactic that can be clearly seen in representations of the crisis-woman. If it is true, as Jacques Derrida maintains, that the "'representation' of crisis, and the rhetoric that it organizes, always have at the end this goal: to identify, in order to limit, a more serious and formless threat, in reality without shape and without norm," then one of the central concerns of this study is to reach a better understanding of the so-called formless threat embodied by the *donna-crisi* and thus to reach a better understanding of the operations of fascist ideology as a whole.[9] The first step in this process, however, is to reach a better understanding of the *donna-crisi* herself.

The Origins and Emergence of the Crisis-Woman

Although the crisis-woman was a figure of fascist propaganda that emerged and subsequently disappeared in the early 1930s, her origins can be traced back at least to the previous decade when rapidly evolving gender roles were particularly visible in popular culture, especially in the world of fashion. The figure that perhaps best represents this rapid evolution is the iconic 1920s figure of the modern woman – the American flapper, the French *garçonne*, or the German *neue frau*, for example – who cut across a variety of cultures.

The modern woman emerged in Europe and the United States (as well as non-Western countries) as a result of social, political, and cultural changes that came to a head at the start of the new century. In Italy, one might identify three major factors that contribute to her emergence: the experience and aftermath of the Great War, the nation's increased rate of industrialization and urbanization, and the rapid growth of consumerism and mass culture. As a result of these factors women occupied a more visible position in the public sphere and in the workforce – often, it must be noted, out of economic necessity rather than any profound desire to improve the condition of women per se. In addition, on a sociocultural front the emergence of the modern woman was no doubt supported by the marked strengthening in these years of Italian feminist campaigns and other emancipatory movements. Although these emancipatory groups were quite diverse in their philosophies and goals, they often shared overarching concerns for issues such as suffrage, the admission of women to higher education, wage equity, and support for mothers and pregnant women.[10] It is easy to imagine not only how the modern woman was a decidedly positive figure for many such groups, but also how the newly established fascist regime may have found her threatening.

The fashionable, cosmopolitan modern woman of the 1920s was visually characterized by what we now call "classic twenties style": short dresses with a hemline at the knee, dropped waistlines that deemphasized the hips, and a flattened bust that diminished the curves of the breasts (Figure 2). The vocabulary of 1920s high fashion favoured sleek minimalism over ornamentation, and as a result the female silhouette appeared smooth and almost geometrical. What was significant about the radical reshaping of women's dress in this decade, however, was that it implied a corollary reshaping of the female body. As historian of dress and costume Valerie Steele describes, the female physical ideal of the 1920s was "the thin, young woman, who was so far from symbolizing the family that her dress minimized the maternal bosom, while exposing the legs, in the manner of a little girl."[11] This youthful style was often complemented by a short, boyish haircut like the famed Eton crop. Also popular was the cloche hat, which mimicked short hair in its close-fitting shape. Finally, the use of cosmetics to artificially enhance natural beauty was a must. As historian Grazietta Butazzi describes, the face was to be "rendered static by painting the mouth and eyes" [reso fisso dal trucco della bocca e degli occhi] and "in its desired mask-like theatricality, it recalled various phenomena of the day: from abstract art, to cinema, to the sensational discovery of the Egyptian mummies" [nella voluta teatralità da maschera non risulta estraneo ad alcune delle esperienze del momento, dall'arte astratta al cinematografo, alla sensazionale scoperta delle mummie egiziane].[12] The appeal of this transgressive modern woman was seemingly

più suggestivo potrebbe aver inventato la moda per illeggiadrire un viso femminile. E questa moda infatti, da tempo si ripete e ritorna sin dalle epoche più lontane. Basta guardare una galleria di quadri antichi per esserne convinti.

Maria Antonietta non è forse dipinta con un «fichu» di mussola bianca sulle spalle nel noto quadro della «Vigée - Lebrun»? L'Imperatrice Eugenia e la bella Contessa di Castiglione non sono forse riprodotte con un «fichu» incrociato sul petto?

Nel corredo di Bianca Maria Sforza sono menzionati quattro «fichus» di tulle bianco, e, narrano le storie, che madame de Pompadour, o meglio, madame d'Etoiles, portava una vaporosa sciarpa di tulle bianco sulle spalle quando Luigi XV la scorse per la prima volta.

PER LA FRESCA GIOVINEZZA CHE SBOCCIA NELLE NOSTRE CASE LE VACANZE SONO IL RAGGIUNGIMENTO DI UNA META SOGNATA

Abito in shantung naturale a impunture rosa, la scollatura ... bordata in bianco. Cappello in paglia con fiori.

Abito da tennis in grossa tela ..., senza maniche con piccolo gilet di mussola bianca.

Abito da pomeriggio bleu pastel chiarissimo la cui sottana s'allarga sui davanti con un fascio di pieghe. La giacca senza maniche è in ... bleuet.

Due semplici abitini. L'uno in mousseline cerise a grandi pieghe con pois ...; l'altro in grossa tela celestina e sweater in lana.

Figure 2. A drawing showing examples of classic twenties style, published in *Sovrana* (June 1927). The title reads: "For the fresh youthfulness that is blossoming in our fashion houses, vacation is a dream come true." From left to right the figures show "two simple dresses" for young girls, a sleeveless "tennis outfit," "a dress in *shantung* [rough silk]" with a "straw hat," and "a pastel blue afternoon dress" with a "sleeveless jacket." (By permission of the Biblioteca Nazionale Braidense, Milan. Reproduction prohibited.)

uncontainable – not only at the start of the fascist regime but throughout – and she regularly appeared in the venues of popular culture such as magazines, store window displays, films, and pulp novels despite the regime's attempts to squelch her.[13]

I have delineated the stereotypical physical and visual traits of the modern woman for demonstrative purposes, but it is important to keep in mind that the modern woman was not so much a coherent figure with a narrowly circumscribed set of attributes as a condensation of transgressive female types that varied according to historical context.[14] As an amalgamation of types, the Italian modern woman, like her counterparts in other countries, could be depicted as a white-collar office worker, an athlete, or an activist. She took up activities that were traditionally coded as male: she might be seen driving a car at top speed leaving behind a rising trail of dust; she might be seen posing at the end of her transatlantic solo flight; she might have worn pants; she might have smoked in public. But whatever her occupation or pastime, she had a distinct personality characterized by traditionally "masculine" traits; as Whitney Chadwick and Tirza True Latimer succinctly put it: "She was in control, self-assured, capable, aggressive, adventurous, independent."[15]

Enthusiastic commentators in the 1920s saw this iconic figure as cutting-edge, youthful, and playfully androgynous. Indignant detractors saw her as an abnormally masculinized and misguided fad. The regime, however, was even more strident in its views: it saw the modern woman as a dangerous figure, particularly for the ways in which her body was most often represented as lithe and slim in order to conform to the sleek, minimalist fashions of the 1920s; she was the embodiment of a threat both to a woman's biological ability to bear healthy children and to her social inclination to do so, and therefore was a threat to the nation as a whole. The regime tried to attenuate the appeal of the modern woman first by generating female types designed to compete with her and second, in the early 1930s, by launching a counter-figure: the unpalatable and abject crisis-woman.

Although from its inception fascism privileged a traditional, maternal, earthy, and domestic image of woman, it also consciously generated nationalist images of modern women such as the *nuova italiana* or the *accademista*. These were intended to compete with the attractive, more cosmopolitan images of modern women that were contemporaneously circulating throughout the country. Fascist representations of the modern woman were conceived in the vein of the *uomo nuovo* as part of the larger project of creating a new Italy. I discuss fascist images of the modern woman in more detail in chapter 1, but suffice it to say here that a variety of models of femininity vied for the public's attention not just in the 1920s but throughout the two decades of fascist rule: the *fascist* woman (whether more traditional or more modern) often existed side by side with the *non-fascist* cosmopolitan modern woman (who took on many different forms). Hereafter, to distinguish the fascist modern women from the non-fascist type, the term "modern woman" will be used exclusively to refer to the non-fascist, cosmopolitan modern woman, whereas the terms *"donna nuova"* and *"nuova italiana"* will refer to fascist expressions of the modern woman. It was in the context of these competing and contrasting figures that the crisis-woman was born.

The term *"donna-crisi"* was coined by fascist ideologues as part of a campaign against what they considered to be "unhealthy" non-fascist images of modern women (as opposed to those that were fascist and therefore healthy). Historian Natalia Aspesi discusses the emergence of the term in her writing on fashion under the regime. She observes that when journalist Gaetano Polverelli took up his new position as head of Mussolini's Press Office in 1931 he made the following declaration: "The fascist woman must be physically healthy to be able to become the mother of healthy children ... Therefore, to be absolutely eliminated are sketches of artificially thin and masculine female figures who represent the type of sterile woman of decadent western civilization" [La donna fascista deve essere fisicamente sana, per poter diventare madre di figli sani ... Vanno quindi assolutamente eliminati i disegni di figure femminili artificiosamente dimagrate e mascolinizzate, che rappresentano il tipo di donna sterile della decadente civiltà occidentale].[16] Polverelli named this "artificially thin," "masculine," and "sterile" modern woman the *"donna-crisi,"* and called for the publication of short articles, stories, and other items denouncing her.[17] Over the next few years a series of *veline* or press circulars (named after the thin paper on which they were printed) reminded journalists of their duty to condemn the crisis-woman regularly in their publications. This resulted in a spate of allusions to the *donna-crisi* in the early 1930s that petered out after a few years.

It is essential to view Polverelli's dictate within the larger context of a fascist backlash against the iconic image of the cosmopolitan modern woman of the 1920s.[18] What distinguished the *donna-crisi*, however, was the fact that she was strategically designed to emphasize one specific aspect of the modern woman: her extremely thin body. When Polverelli declared that the Italian press should publish articles and stories against the *donna-crisi,* his intention may very well have been twofold: first, to reduce the modern woman – who was an amalgam figure with varying powerful expressions – to a single characteristic and in doing so make her a type that could more easily be controlled; and second, to recast the modern woman as an exclusively negative or abject figure by associating her with the notion of crisis, which in the early 1930s evoked *la grande crisi,* or the grim economic crisis of these years.

It is important to note that the simplified, exaggerated, propagandistic figure of the *donna-crisi* was substantially bolstered by the ways in which fascist culture – not to mention the culture of early twentieth-century Italy in general – was obsessed with a fundamentally positivist desire to measure and quantify the human body and categorize bodies into easily comprehensible types; this was especially true of the deviant body. Lombroso's school of positivist criminological theory, which argued that the morphology of the body could reveal a predisposition to delinquent behaviour, was particularly influential in this regard, and echoes of this strain of thought are evident in many responses to Polverelli's dictate – even those that are far from scientific in nature. (In chapter 2 I discuss more fully the central role of scientific discourse with regard to the formation and appeal of the crisis-woman.)

Polverelli's dictate, which identifies the thin body as the defining characteristic of the *donna-crisi,* reveals much more than the crisis-woman's origins as a backlash figure against classic twenties style. It also points to fascism's preoccupation with the healthy female body and to the larger historical context that must frame any account of the origins of the crisis-woman, that is, fascist body politics as they were put forth in the demographic campaign.

In 1927 – two years after the founding of the regime and just as classic twenties style peaked – Mussolini launched one of his first major social campaigns, the *battaglia demografica* or "demographic battle," as it was often called. This war of sorts consisted of a series of pronatalist measures, directed primarily at women, which were designed to "improve the race" and boost the nation's population from forty to sixty million within twenty years. A good indication of how far-fetched this goal actually was is the fact that, according to Italy's National Bureau of Statistics, Italy fell just short of the Duce's number in 2012 with a resident population of 59,685,227.[19]

Although women were particularly targeted, the demographic campaign was in theory concerned with the normalization of productive sexuality and productive bodies for all Italians. With this goal in mind, the regime enacted a host of political and legislative measures. Among the most well known are the financial awards for prolific families; other measures included tax exemptions for married couples and large families, family allowances, marriage bonuses, low-interest birth and marriage loans, maternity insurance, and preferment in hiring and promotion for those with large families. Such "positive" measures to encourage nuptiality and fertility went hand in hand with a lesser number of repressive or "negative" measures designed to further the same end. The regime enacted a tax on bachelorhood and criminalized objects and acts that offended public decency. There was debate on the validity of premarital medical exams designed to protect against hereditary disease, and although they never became obligatory such exams were often unofficially encouraged. Finally, both abortion as well as the dissemination of information on contraceptive measures became punishable crimes against the state.[20] Productive bodies, then, were to be the norm in Italy, and production was to be understood in the widest sense in that reproduction (i.e., increasing the number of Italians in the world) was meant to facilitate the fascist expansion of territory and political power. As Mussolini famously asserted in his Ascension Day speech – which inaugurated the demographic campaign and which I discuss in chapter 4 – Italy's declining birth rate could lead to disastrous consequences: "If we grow smaller, ladies and gentlemen, we won't create an empire, we'll become a colony!" [Se si diminuisce, signori, non si fa l'impero, si diventa una colonia!].[21]

When considering the intensified normalization of so-called "healthy" and productive female sexuality that marked these years, we must also take into account the position of the Catholic Church – especially since it sometimes clashed and sometimes converged with that of the regime. The 1930 encyclical on the sanctity of marriage, "Casti Connubii," written by Pope Pius XI, is a well-known and influential instance of the convergence of church and state with regard to the fascist ideal of the fertile woman. Yet at the same time Catholic culture presented the potential for a certain dissonance with the body politics of the regime, since the thin female body has historically been one of the key exemplars of idealized and desirable female religiosity, as Caroline Walker Bynum for one has pointed out.[22] The thin female body in the Catholic paradigm, however, represents saintliness rather than sterility, thus diverging from fascist semiotics and further underscoring the need for the regime's control of the meaning of this body type. Indeed, the crisis-woman emerged precisely as a figure that helped to shape, control, and discipline the female body and women's behaviour in these years.

In naming the *donna-crisi* Polverelli and his staff must be credited with what would today be called a savvy marketing technique. In the early 1930s, when the *donna-crisi* emerged on the cultural scene, fascist Italy was a country suffering the effects of *la grande crisi*. The national unemployment rate peaked between 1931 and 1934, and the agricultural sector that drove the country was hit especially hard.[23] The impact of the worldwide economic collapse was so strongly felt in the daily lives of Italians that a new buzzword was on the lips of the nation; the word "crisis" suddenly became wildly popular. Mussolini's Press Office, under the direction of Polverelli, astutely took advantage of this popularity when choosing an epithet for the unhealthily thin modern woman that it wished to eliminate.

One finds evidence of Italy's larger "crisis craze" in divergent fields of cultural production. In 1933, for example, singer Rodolfo De Angelis created a national sensation when he introduced a new tune poking fun at the exaggerated use of the word, entitled "So, What's This Crisis?" [Mah, cos'è questa crisi?].[24] Earlier, in May 1932, a writer for the popular magazine *Excelsior* exclaimed: "It's a bit the craze of our times: the crisis is the cause of everything. Because of the crisis our shoes leak, we catch a cold, we yawn at the theatre, we don't digest cake, and kids are failed at school. Even when an old man points out that a young boy is very small for his age, the latter replies: 'It's the crisis, sir! It's not my fault!'" [È un po' la mania dell' epoca: si attribuisce alla crisi tutto: la crisi, perché le scarpe fanno acqua, perché vengono i raffreddori, perché a teatro si sbadiglia, perché non si digerisce la torta, perché a scuola i ragazzi son bocciati. Lo diceva anche quel bambino al quale un vecchio signore osservava che era molto piccolo per la sua età: "È la crisi, signore! Io non ne ho la colpa!"].[25] In 1933 Jodont, the maker of a popular brand of toothpaste, took advantage of the crisis craze to publish an advertisement in which two men speak to each other about the economic collapse. One laments: "Because of this crisis, I always have a bitter taste in my mouth" [Con questa crisi non faccio che masticare amaro]. The other responds: "Use JODONT. Thanks to it you'll always have healthy, clean teeth and a pleasant taste in your mouth" [Usa l'JODONT. Grazie ad esso avrai sempre i denti sani e puliti, e in bocca un sapore gradevole].[26]

Fashion designers, too, used the crisis craze to their advantage. In September 1931 *Lidel* published an article describing the simple fashions of the upcoming winter season as a type of "crisis" fashion characterized by solemn colours and the frugal use of luxurious trimmings like fur. The author writes in a playfully fatigued tone: "It pains me to start with a tale that for months and months has been waved about like an ominous scarecrow before our hopes and dreams. Nevertheless, I must begin this article with the word crisis, which resounds today in every corner of the earth and must be pronounced each time one alludes to any type of human activity. A crisis, therefore, in the world of fashion" [Mi duole di iniziare con una parabola che da mesi e mesi viene agitata come una spauracchio davanti a tutti i nostri sogni e alle nostre speranze, pure devo mettere in testa a questo articolo la parola crisi che risuona oggi in ogni angolo della terra e che deve essere pronunciata ogni volta che si alluda a qualsiasi forma dell'umana attività. Crisi dunque anche nel campo della moda].[27]

Although talk of a *moda-crisi* [crisis-style] in the fashion world referred to the austere styles of the winter of 1931, the term *donna-crisi* was not used, as one might think, to refer to a woman wearing these depression-era fashions.[28] On the contrary, the term began to appear in fashion magazines immediately after Polverelli's mandate and was used in complete accordance with its charge: a *donna-crisi* was to be understood, quite simply, as the type of modern woman who obstinately and dangerously insisted on the extraordinarily thin figure that had been popular in the previous decade. What the fascist regime wanted to stress with the idea of the crisis-woman was the dissolution of the seductive aura of emancipation, transgression, and youthfulness that once belonged to this sleek, modern, thin woman. The crisis-woman was a figure designed to link thinness with darker associations, such as deprivation and hardship, that were more relevant to the current moment and were being felt by nearly all of Italy's population. Aided by the crisis-craze happening on a linguistic and cultural level together with the *grande crisi* happening on an economic level, the *donna-crisi* was a figure that quickly caught on in a variety of fields.

Organization of This Book

In order to flesh out as fully as possible the multiple facets of the figure of the *donna-crisi*, each chapter of this book concentrates on a different discursive field. The first three chapters focus on fields in which representations of the crisis-woman most commonly appear: chapter 1 on fashion, chapter 2 on science, and chapter 3 on satire. These three chapters contain the majority of new primary sources on the *donna-crisi*, and my hope is that they will be especially useful to scholars working on representations of femininity in this period. These first chapters privilege the historical and symptomatic reading of the crisis-woman that I describe above; in other words, they provide a reading that considers the figure in relation to the changing social and cultural terrain. Chapter 4 focuses instead on political texts and fleshes out a rhetorical and ideological reading of the crisis-woman that is nascent in the first three chapters. The concluding chapter briefly describes the decline of the crisis-woman and outlines her legacy. Each chapter, while focused on a specific field, advances the central arguments of the book.

Because fashion is one of the three main discursive fields in which the *donna-crisi* most commonly appears, chapter 1 examines a series of primary texts focusing on women's fashions. These texts directly or indirectly evoke the crisis-woman, are primarily verbal rather than visual, and are taken from a variety of popular women's magazines, including *Lidel, Lei, Amica,* and *Il giornale della donna.* The chapter is divided into two main sections and presents several arguments that are developed in subsequent chapters. First, I analyse representations of the modern woman published in the mid-1920s, that is preceding the birth of the crisis-woman. My discussion questions the common association between "modern" and "subversive," arguing that although representations of the fashionable modern woman may outwardly stress revolutionary ideals such as the dismantling of the "natural" boundaries of the female body, in fact such representations are much more complex and multivalent than often acknowledged. My close reading shows that these images express profound anxiety about revolutionary ideals at the same time that they advance them, and should therefore be seen as an integral part of fascist structures of power rather than as points of resistance that lie beyond the reach of that power. My larger argument, which I underscore in the following chapters, is that depictions of the modern woman encourage disciplinary surveillance and bodily control, and set the stage for the appearance of the propaganda figure of the crisis-woman in the 1930s. The second part of the chapter focuses not on precursors but on direct representations of the crisis-woman in fascist dictates and in women's magazines in order to highlight the congruence between the semiotics of the female body in both sets of images. Overall, the chapter advances a historical and symptomatic reading of the crisis-woman; I show that the regime launched the negative figure of the *donna-crisi* in an attempt to control modern and rapidly evolving ideas about gender and the female body that were deeply rooted in the world of popular fashion and that had the potential to undermine fascist ideals.

Chapter 2 moves to the second discursive field in which one commonly finds representations of the *donna-crisi*: the authoritative discourse of science. The texts I examine here can be divided into two groups. First, I examine the specialized scientific writings of one particular fascist scientist, Nicola Pende, whose research about the negative repercussions of thinness on women's health was influential far beyond the medical field. Second, I look at a series of articles on the crisis-woman – published in the socio-scientific journal *Maternità ed infanzia* [*Maternity and Infancy*] – which present a type of hybrid between specialized scientific writing and popular journalism. Taken together, these texts illustrate not only how popular depictions of the *donna-crisi* were profoundly influenced by the perceived authority of scientific discourse, but also how they drew on a legacy of nineteenth-century scientific thought, and in particular positivist thought, which advanced the notion that cultural signs of deviance become knowable and legible first and foremost as exterior symptoms of bodily disease. In order to clarify this last point I focus throughout the chapter on the abject pathological body as a locus for the production of knowledge and power. Here I build on the idea introduced in chapter 1 that the *donna-crisi* was a figure strategically used by the regime to incite surveillance and control of the female body. On a larger scale, this chapter presents a historical and symptomatic reading of the crisis-woman that not only highlights her association with various perceived threats related to shifts in Italy's social and demographic landscape – threats such as sexual deviance, racial decline, or moral degeneration – but also shows how that association was solidified by the regime's strategic employment of scientific discourse.

Chapter 3 examines the last major discursive field in which one commonly finds representations of the crisis-woman: satirical cartoons. The chapter begins with a close reading of the signifying mechanisms driving the humour of these popular cartoons – for example, the discursive objectification of the crisis-woman and the subsequent normalization of bodily ideals. I argue that these satirical cartoons are an excellent example of a subtle type of fascist propaganda, which philosopher Jacques Ellul calls the "propaganda of integration," that encourages a type of hegemonizing humour in line with the regime's ideals. One might say that rather than concentrating on disciplinary surveillance at the level of the body, this chapter focuses on disciplinary surveillance at the level of the mind. In my close readings I explore more deeply a variety of themes introduced in the previous two chapters, such as the relation between the crisis-woman and the threat of sexual deviance, or between the crisis-woman and racial degeneration. In keeping with my overarching interest in the multivalent operations of power, the last section of this chapter complicates my reading of these cartoons as examples of propaganda and asks to what extent they might inadvertently present a subversion of fascist ideals. As in the previous two chapters, this chapter presents a historical and symptomatic reading of the crisis-woman that is attentive to social anxieties produced by changing gender roles, shifting class lines, and permeable racial boundaries.

Chapter 4 marks a shift in the book insofar as it draws out and further develops the rhetorical and ideological reading embedded in the first three chapters. In the first section of this chapter I reframe the texts discussed in the previous three chapters through my reading of the *donna-crisi* as a figure of ideological fantasy. Drawing in particular on the work of Slavoj Žižek, I argue that the crisis-woman does not simply reflect major changes in Italy's social and demographic landscape but in fact serves a crucial function within fascist ideology: she is a figure onto which the antagonisms of modern Italian society could be displaced, masked, and resolved – that is, at least in appearance. In addition to fleshing out the mechanisms through which the *donna-crisi* masked antagonisms and upheld fascist fantasies about the integrity of the Italian nation, I also explore the ways in which the crisis-woman points to the untenability of these fantasies, and consider the extent to which she might be understood as an oppositional figure. In the second part of the chapter I link the figure of the crisis-woman to a broader discussion of the workings of the concept of crisis in fascist ideology as a whole. Using as my primary texts a series of Mussolini's political speeches that invoke crisis – and particularly demographic crisis – I show how the notion of crisis was strategically put to multiple uses: first, it validated a series of legislative and political actions such as those associated with the demographic campaign; second, it validated the larger enterprise of "fascistization" (i.e., turning every level and type of activity – from the most insignificant private decision to the most visible public display – into an activity in service of the regime); and third, it masked any internal threats to that enterprise.

In the concluding chapter I discuss the decline of representations of the crisis-woman and ask why this figure – who appeared so briefly in the early 1930s – is still so fascinating to scholars and the general public. Although this study does not pretend to undertake the impossible task of offering an exhaustive picture and understanding of the crisis-woman, I hope that readers find my investigation of these new sources thorough and that my interpretations stimulate further discussion about the inscription of power on the gendered body in Italy during the years of the regime and beyond.

1

The Donna-crisi and the Fashion World: From Revolution to Regulatory Ideal

As we saw above, there emerged in the 1920s in Italy and Europe "not only a new fashion but also a new physical ideal" which envisioned the female body in a manner that radically broke with the past.[1] Fashion trends began to shift away from the long-established maternal archetype as the once-popular curvaceous Edwardian figure was replaced by an idealized "slender and sinuous body type with smaller breasts, slimmer hips, and long legs."[2] Women were cutting their hair, wearing pants, and smoking in public. In short, women were becoming "modern," that is to say, representative of a new century and a new way of being.

Among the Italian authors who depict the modern woman during the fascist period, one stands out in particular: the popular writer and journalist Irene Brin who, in her contemporary reflections on the *ventennio,* paints a picture of women's lives that decidedly goes against the grain of fascist ideals. Her writing is devoid of any reference to the iconic housewife with happy children scampering at her feet or to the *nuova italiana*. Instead, Brin describes another type of woman – a much more worldly and fashionable woman. In her collection of essays *Usi e costumi 1920–1940* [*Customs and Habits 1920–1940*] she says the following about the Italian woman of the mid-twenties:

> Season by season women fell in love with their liberty, with their modesty. Moreover, absolute personal satisfaction animated every single aspect of social life, and short almost stark dresses were underscored by the incredible brashness of those who wore them. A fat string of Japanese pearls, a mad flower on the shoulder, a *chiffon* handkerchief tied to the wrist … these were the only ornaments admitted by women who swore to

emancipate themselves from the hat, who substituted silk stockings for socks, and replaced sandals for shoes.

> Stagione per stagione, le donne si innamoravano della loro libertà, della loro modestia. Del resto un'assoluta soddisfazione personale animava ogni particolare aspetto della vita sociale, e le vesti corte, rudimentali, venivano sottolineate dalla baldanza incredibile di chi le indossava. Un grosso filo di perle giapponesi, un fiore apoplettico alla spalla, un fazzoletto di *chiffon* legato al polso [...] costituivano i solo ornamenti ammessi dalla donne che giuravano di volersi emancipare dal cappellino, e sostituivano le calze con le calzettine, le scarpe con i sandali.[3]

This passage shows us that although the mid-twenties were marked by growing restrictions on women's individual liberties and social roles as the fascist regime consolidated its power – perhaps hinted at in Brin's insistence on "modesty" – these were also years of relative freedom. Brin's colourful picture of "absolute personal satisfaction" contrasts sharply with the fascist notion that women should be modest to the point of being homely – a notion that Carlalberto Grillenzoni would later sum up in his 1933 statistical essay on fashion and demography. A committed fascist, social scientist, and pupil of Corrado Gini, Grillenzoni dryly warns of the dire consequences of a woman's exaggerated preoccupation with style: "although excessive attention to one's own elegance may slightly increase the probability of marriage, *it is also the greatest of obstacles opposed to fertility* [l'eccessiva cura della propria eleganza, se avvanteggia di ben poco le probabilità matrimoniali, *è invece il più forte degli ostacoli opposti a la fecondità*] (266; emphasis added).[4] In Grillenzoni's eyes, a modern woman like the one described by Brin might be much like the *donna-crisi* insofar as her attention to the latest fashions threatened her reproductive capacities and could put the health of the nation at risk. But as Brin's image illustrates, a wide variety of non-hegemonic modern female types thrived during the fascist period – primarily in the artefacts of mass and consumer culture, and particularly in those whose target audience was women. Indeed, as critic Elisabetta Mondello observes: "In magazines and periodicals for women, the 'new woman,' which fascism hoped would be 'an exemplary wife and mother,' ... is polarized by cultural models that do not coincide with the regime's official image."[5]

I begin this chapter by considering a series of primary texts that describe the modern woman and focus in particular on the revolutionary fashion trends that she espoused and embodied. I have organized the material of this section in a loosely chronological manner, and I purposely limit my discussion to representations published in women's magazines because, as Mondello notes, the models of femininity they present often markedly go against the "positive" models advanced by the regime. I have chosen these texts in order to stress the semiotic complexity and volatility of representations of the modern woman and show that understanding her exclusively as a revolutionary figure who stands in opposition to "positive" fascist types is a problematic and reductive gesture.

Circumscribing 1920s Fashion

In May 1925, the Italian fashion magazine *Lidel* published an article entitled "The First Warmth of Summer, The First Light Clothing" ["Primi tepori estivi, primi abiti leggeri"] in which the author, in the opening paragraph, describes the liberated modern woman as follows:

> Comparing the models of yesterday with those of today, one measures in a glance the progress made in less than half a century. Thanks most likely to tennis, golf, and the other sporting games that predominate nowadays, one sees nothing but thin, lithe, and precise figures in fashion magazines. The short skirt reigns, sleeves are antiquated, the rigid bust of long ago has been substituted by a simple band of diaphanous silk muslin which reveals the palpitating harmony of every movement of the body. It seems that the female figure itself has been transformed.

> A confrontare i modelli d'allora con gli odierni, si misura con uno sguardo l'evoluzione compiuta in meno di mezzo secolo. Grazie probabilmente al tennis, al golf, ed agli altri giuochi sportivi che ora prevalgono, non si vedono più nei giornali di moda che profili snelli, sciolti, precisi. La gonna corta trionfa, le maniche sono antiquate, il busto rigido di una volta è sostituito da una semplice benda di mussolina diafana di seta che rivela la palpitante armonia di ogni movimento del corpo. Sembra che le stesse linee femminili si siano trasformate.[6]

By implicitly equating the "transformation" of the "female figure" with women's political and social emancipation – the "progress made in less than half a century" – the author, who uses only the pseudonym "Mag," suggests that it is not just fashion that has evolved but woman herself: the 1920s woman is independent and physically active; her dress is simple and practically suited to her modern lifestyle; without scruples, she sensuously reveals her body by wearing diaphanous clothing and by exposing her arms and legs; she is a new woman, and decidedly *not* the new woman championed by the fascist regime since the signs of motherhood, domesticity, or political allegiance are nowhere to be found. Published at a unique moment in the fascist period – after the establishment of the regime but before the institution of the most repressive policies against women – this article sums up classic twenties style and the revolution it represented in a few pithy words.

Lidel was one of the most prominent of a handful of refined Italian fashion magazines to appear during the height of these controversial fashion trends, and it featured transformative modern styles while simultaneously emphasizing nationalistic ideals.[7] Founded by Lydia De Liguoro and debuting in 1919, *Lidel* unsurprisingly came out of Milan, the most cosmopolitan of Italy's cities and an emergent fashion capital. The article demonstrates in an exemplary manner the fact that even forward-looking expressions of modern fashion made substantive use of normative thinking about women and women's bodies, which was the basis for fascist ideals. Indeed, I will argue that the author's apparent ambition, expressed in this opening paragraph, to undertake a radical exploration, reconstruction, and reconstitution of the female body is attenuated by an underlying sense of anxiety about this project and an insistent return to the language of moderation and control. The multivalence of an outwardly progressive narrative such as this is typical of many similar contemporary publications, and it enables a subtle shift away from the revolutionary aspects of modern dress in order to bring it more in line with hegemonic fascist thought.

There are three vignettes in the article that inflect the opening description of the progressive modern woman, and the first shows clearly just how this subtle shift happens. When speaking of the fashions of the day, the author recounts the following story as it had been told to her:

> A young lady, at lunch in an elegant *trattoria*, stains the front of her dress and tries in vain to wipe off the remains of the sauce clearly visible on the light fabric. Irritated, she disappears for a few minutes and returns looking immaculate. To what sovereign remedy did she turn? To the simplest one: she removed her dress and put it on backwards. If some indiscreet person had raised the scarf gently draped on her back, he would have seen the oily stain there. With today's fashions, metamorphosis becomes easy.

> Una giovane signora, a pranzo in una trattoria elegante, si macchia il vestito sul davanti e cerca invano di fare scomparire le tracce della salsa, molto visibili sulla stoffa chiara. Irritata, si eclissa per alcuni minuti e torna immacolata. A quale rimedio sovrano aveva ricorso? Al più semplice: si era tolta il vestito e se l'era infilato alla rovescia: se qualche indiscreto avesse sollevato la sciarpa mollemente allentata sul dorso vi avrebbe riveduto la macchia d'unto. Con le mode attuali la metamorfosi diventa facile.[8]

While this vignette vaunts the appeal of the easy, practical metamorphosis made possible by the fashions of the day, it also expresses a profound anxiety about those same features. This is a story about "purity and danger," to use the language of Mary Douglas.[9] The colours are morally charged, as a dark "stain" on a "light fabric" is erased. This charge is linked to the institution of the church through the use of religious language: after recourse to a "sovereign" remedy, the lady reappears in "immaculate" form. Indeed, the metamorphosis suggested has echoes of the miraculous changes to the female body that are typical of hagiographic narratives.[10] The reader, however, knows that the stain has not been erased but merely displaced; it is still there on the "back" of the woman's dress. Instead, what has been erased are the traditional signs of sexual difference: the dress is cut the same in front and behind so that it hangs uniformly flat on both sides and does not suggest a woman's anatomical difference from a man.

This modern flexible dress, which can be turned from front to back or even – one can imagine – inside out, suggests a similar uncanny flexibility of the modern female body. Indeed, the author's allusion to an "easy" metamorphosis – a process by which one body becomes another – further emphasizes the implied connection between dress and body. As anthropologist Ted Polhemus argues, dress should be considered an extension of the body:

> Can we really assume that the limits and boundaries of the human body itself are obvious? Does "the body" end with the skin or should we include hair, nails? … What of bodily waste materials? … Surely the decorative body arts such as tattooing, scarification, cranial modification and body painting should also be considered … [and] it has been shown that it is insignificant (if not inaccurate) to sharply differentiate between bodily decoration and adornment on the one hand and the clothing of the body on the other.[11]

This vignette, then, outwardly proposes a radical new subjectivity for women, one that is not rooted in "anatomical destiny" but is more flexible and can be transformed simply with a change of dress. In short, it proposes a cultural configuration of sex and gender that denaturalizes the relation between the two and flies in the face of fascist ideals.

At the conclusion of this story, however, the powerful metamorphosis described by the author is attenuated, as the suggestive "stain" of sexual difference – which metonymically stands for the female body and its identifying fluids – cannot be erased. The stain is revealed as soon as a small piece of fabric is lifted. Similarly, the hidden "truth" of the woman's body – that is, of her female sex – can be revealed by lifting her unsexed clothes. In the end, this vignette overturns a normative association between gender and sex only to reinforce it, since the body is decidedly figured as separate from dress: one remains embedded in the unchanging rock of the natural while the other is a cultural caprice and a passing fad. In the end, the lesson suggested by this anecdote seems to be that one can praise the practicality of modern fashions so long as one does not assume that the female body can also be reshaped. Typical of women's fashion magazines of the day, this article in *Lidel* vaunts the modern "transformation" of the female figure, while at the same time making clear that this transformation has its limits. Modern fashion may suggest revolutionary ideas, but these ideas cannot and should not fundamentally alter the reality (the sex) of the female body.

I should note here that the author of this article makes ample use of the vignette – designed to be read either as an anecdotal gossipy snippet of overheard conversation or as the eyewitness retelling of a riveting event – in order to characterize her narrative as "realistic if not real" [verosimile se non vero].[12] But the reader must not be drawn into this pretense of verisimilitude since the vignette relies heavily on literary tropes and rhetorical constructions and in doing so calls out to be read critically with attention to such devices. This type of analysis is especially important because narratives from magazines like *Lidel* figure prominently in scholarly work, and yet so little has been written about the rhetorical devices they employ.[13]

The second vignette in this article takes as its subject not clothing but hair and focuses on another major threat posed by new fashion trends, namely the manner in which they imply the reorganization of both bodily and social space. The narrator recounts:

> And so it happened that an acquaintance of mine found himself in a well-known hairdresser's shop where the men passively submit to the scissors, the razor, and the vigorous massaging of the staff. Suddenly, a woman enters and everyone assumes that she is going to look for someone she knows, but she confidently moves toward an empty chair and asks the hairdresser – who can barely conceal his surprise – for a cut. He seats her, puts a white cape over her, offers her a newspaper to read, and begins working his scissors. When he is finished, according to the habit formed with male clients, he asks if she would like a rub-down. In response to an affirmative nod, he pours cologne water on her head and vigorously massages it. The lady then gets up, pays, and exits with the greatest nonchalance, as if she were walking out of any common shop.

> Così è capitato ad un mio conoscente di trovarsi in un grande negozio da parrucchiere ove gli uomini si sottopongono docilmente alle forbici, al rasojo o al massaggio vigoroso dei commessi. D'improvviso, si vede entrare una signora e tutti presumono che vada a cercare qualche persona amica, ma ella si dirige con disinvoltura verso un seggiolone vuoto e al commesso che nasconde a stento il suo stupore chiede di tagliarle i capelli. Il commesso la fa sedere, le pone indosso un accappatoio bianco, le offre un giornale da leggere e agita le forbici. Quando ha finito, secondo l'abitudine presa coi clienti maschili, le domanda se vuole una frizione e ad un cenno affermativo le versa l'acqua di Colonia sul capo e gliela strofina con vigoria. Poi la signora si alza, paga e se ne va con la massima indifferenza, come se uscisse da un negozio qualsiasi.[14]

Like the first vignette, this second story possesses an unmistakably rebellious tone. Gender roles, however, are subverted even before the virile woman enters the scene, as the men in the shop "passively submit" [si sottopongono docilmente] to the sharp implements and vigorous massaging of the staff. The woman, on the other hand, assumes all the trappings of masculinity: she "confidently moves toward" [si dirige verso] the chair, a place normally reserved for a men; like any male client, she is given a white cape, offered a newspaper, and receives a rub-down; finally, she responds to questions with a brisk nod of the head rather than a polite lady-like reply. Gender roles, partially destabilized in the first vignette, seem in this second one to function as performative rather than normative.[15] But it would be misleading to read this woman as a straightforward symbol of emancipation to be held up as a model for *Lidel's* readers. She is better described as pure spectacle: attractive, comic, and in some respects even pathetic or appalling.

A closer look at the passage shows that the spectacle is not her short hair (which is never described); neither is it the overturning of gender roles (which are upset even before the woman enters the scene). The spectacle is much more specific: it is the woman's transgressive intrusion into a male social space. The female subject in this story has left the bounds of her private, domestic sphere and disrupts the order of the male public sphere. As in the previous vignette about the flexible dress, one notes that the female body is the particular source of disruption. The transgression, however, is not the potential inversion and perversion of the female body as it is in the first vignette; instead it is the distasteful eruption of the female body into a traditionally male space. The desire to contain this body is played out most clearly when the narrator gives the last word of this of the story to a male friend, and the scene shifts from the spectacle of a woman in a men's shop to the spectacle of a woman's toilette:

> If women with cropped hair almost always have a tiny comb in their hand to fix their hair, even in restaurants, it means that there is something wrong with the fashion trend. Elegant young women have already taken to beautifying themselves in public with curls and cosmetics: now they're even using combs. "When will they start using toothbrushes?" asks an irreverent (male) friend of mine.
>
> Se le donne dai capelli recisi hanno quasi sempre un minuscolo pettine in mano per ravviarsi le chiome anche alla trattoria, vuol dire che la moda lascia a desiderare. Le signorine eleganti avevan già l'abitudine di abbellirsi in pubblico con la cirri e col belletto: ora si servono in pubblico anche del pettine. 'A quando lo spazzolino da denti?' chiede un mio amico irriverente.[16]

Modern fashion has forced grooming out of the dressing room and into the dining room, and comedy – evidenced in the hyperbole of this passage – serves to dissipate the anxiety produced by the shift from private to public. But it is not so much the toilette as the display of the female body that is "wrong with the fashion trend," as the author puts it.

Notably, the body is present in this passage only metonymically, symbolized by the comb, the curled lock of hair, cosmetics, and the toothbrush. With the complicity of her male friend, the narrator rhetorically veils the female body and metonymically hides it from view, thus enacting the modesty that women who make themselves up in public fail to show. Throughout the article, the author resuscitates and relies on typical nineteenth-century literary tropes of the female body that stress defilement, pollution, and disorder. The modest veiling of the body (literal in the first vignette and metonymical in the second) implies the corruption and excess generated by the mere presence of the female body, not coincidentally figured in the first vignette as a "stain." This second vignette, once again, reframes the original revolutionary description of modern fashion trends by suggesting that if they reveal "the palpitating harmony of every movement of the body," then they must always do so within socially acceptable limits.

The third and final vignette, yet again, implicitly warns against the danger of bodily excess posed by modern fashion trends. It focuses on sexuality and serves as a cautionary tale against physical and moral corruption. Moreover, it speaks of the dangerous erasure of class difference enabled by those trends. This vignette tells of a needy peasant girl who attempts to profit from the fad for short hair by selling her long blond tresses. Just as she is about to close the deal with a vendor, a stranger approaches her and offers more than double the price she has negotiated. Naturally, she accepts. The stranger then takes a pair of scissors, cuts a single hair from the girl's head, and carefully places it in his billfold. The narrator recounts how the stranger "paternally" tells the young woman: "Remember, my child … that God gave you this beautiful attribute to make you even more beautiful, and it would be an impious act to destroy it" [Ricordatevi figlia mia, … che Dio vi ha fornito di questo magnifico ornamento per rendervi più bella, e sarebbe un atto di empietà distruggere un ornamento simile].[17]

When the man places the strand of hair into his billfold, he indicates quite literally its commodity value. But hair is not the only commodity in this tale. Hair stands in for the irrepressible sexuality of the female body as a whole, and one can only assume that a woman who will sell her hair for money is one short step away from selling her body.[18] In addition, the religious overtones of this passage are unmistakable.[19] This lower-class girl is in danger not only of corrupting her soul through an "impious act" but also of corrupting her humanity by objectifying her body and turning it into a product for consumption. The "paternal" demeanor of the man, his reference to the young woman as "my child," and his condemnation of her potentially "impious act," all suggest the guidance of a priest. Indeed, this story reads like a biblical parable – a sort of inverse Samson and Delilah story – with God's intention to make the woman "even more beautiful" clearly delineated at the end.

Markers of class also stand out here, and one must remember that this is a story about a peasant told for an audience of primarily bourgeois woman readers. Because the protagonist is from an underprivileged class, *Lidel's* well-to-do readers may have been able to dissociate themselves, at least in part, from the danger of sliding from normal to deviant by cutting one's hair. This threat is present, but it is contained in the lower classes. The female bourgeois reader, however, may well have perceived another danger. If the same fashion can be adopted by all classes, if "metamorphosis becomes easy" with new fashions, then might not the distinction between bourgeois and peasant also be in danger of being erased? As numerous scholars have remarked, the rise of mass and consumer culture in early twentieth-century Italy and Europe provoked anxiety about the elimination of traditional markers of class.[20] Luxury items – from silk stockings to cologne water to radios and even cars – were readily visible for virtual consumption by any woman who turned her gaze to the many magazines on display at the local news-stand or to the growing number of intricately decorated shop windows.[21] Ready-made fashion opened the clothing market to less economically privileged consumers as, for the first time in history, one could easily buy the latest designs straight off the rack rather than having them custom-made by a tailor. The decline of nobility and the bourgeoisie accompanied by the rise of a new middle class made it more difficult to distinguish between blue blood and nouveau riche on the basis of outward appearance. This anxiety about stable class boundaries is clearly expressed in this last vignette, published in a magazine that depended on its bourgeois audience at the same time that it styled itself for mass-market rather than elitist appeal.

In sum, even though *Lidel* was one of the most vociferous promoters of classic twenties style, and even though its pages are filled with revolutionary images of French designs, by no means did the magazine unequivocally celebrate the new styles that came from abroad.[22] Endorsements of these styles were almost invariably accompanied by implicit or explicit calls for moderation and warnings against the dangers of wholeheartedly adopting modern fashion, both of which were completely in line with hegemonic ideals of fascist femininity. Anxieties about changing fashions and gender roles only intensified as the regulation of women's bodies in fascist politics intensified during the 1920s and on into the 1930s. The late 1920s are already marked by a greater focus on women's bodies as a site for the normalization of procreative sexuality as compared to the first part of the decade. In 1925, the health and welfare of many pregnant and nursing mothers began to be overseen by the newly founded ONMI (Opera Nazionale per la Maternità ed Infanzia). In 1927, Mussolini's Ascension Day speech exhorted women to join the so-called battle for births. As I mention above, in 1930 Pope Pius XI inaugurated the new decade with his highly influential encyclical "Casti Connubii," which underscored family values. The encyclical came hot on the heels of the newly proposed Rocco Penal Code, which criminalized abortion, birth control, and even the dissemination of information about contraception. In 1931, Polverelli launched the official campaign against the *donna-crisi*. In 1933, the "Day of the Mother and Child" was established as a day of national celebration. And generally throughout the 1930s, legislation was regularly passed rewarding prolific mothers and discouraging women from working outside the home.

But while we must recognize that images of the modern woman are not necessarily subversive and do not necessarily lie outside the bounds of fascist power, we must also recognize the limitations of fascist power. The conclusion of the first vignette provides a case in point. Although the vignette primarily underscores the normative idea that dress as artifice can neither change nor be exchanged for the nature of the body, a troubling residue remains of the denaturalized relationship between dress and body that is suggested at the story's opening. The author's concern over a flexible, practical, modern dress would be unfounded if the nature of the female body really cannot be changed. Indeed, why shouldn't a woman follow fashions that promote metamorphosis if the sex of her body cannot be put into question? The persistent anxiety articulated in this first vignette and reproduced in those that follow it suggests a persistent threatening disarticulation – summed up in the changing relation between dress and body – of the "natural" relation between femininity and female, between gender and sex, between private and public, between upper class and lower. This disarticulation that refuses to disappear can only relentlessly be *controlled*; and as I will show in the following section, this control is embodied in the figure of the *donna-crisi* that emerges in the 1930s. If we see a proliferation of modern female bodies, types, and identities in women's magazines – despite the rise to power of the fascist regime – then we must also recognize that this proliferation goes hand in hand with the multiplication of techniques to regulate these identities. In sum, women's magazines were a site where the regime exercised both repressive *and* productive power, and it is precisely the multiple operations of power that inform my discussion of the texts in the remainder of this chapter.

The Regime's Figuration of the Crisis-Woman

Before we compare the above descriptions of the modern woman with descriptions of the *donna-crisi* found in publications for a female audience such as *Lidel*, it is helpful to more closely examine the crisis-woman as she is depicted in official communications of the regime, since the latter in large part shaped the former. To this end, I turn to a series of press directives (or *veline*) reproduced by historian Nicola Tranfaglia in his study on communications from the Ministry of Popular Culture (better known as the Minculpop).[23] These documents not only show evidence of a sustained, albeit brief, campaign against the *donna-crisi* in the early 1930s, but also show evidence of the regime's larger attempt to link the figure of the crisis-woman to the more broadly defined modern woman, and in doing so to delineate the contours of an abject modern female body. The campaign against the crisis-woman lasted from 1931 to 1933 and was purportedly designed to banish the "unhealthy" modern woman from the pages of the Italian press. Take for example the following sampling of *veline*, documented by Tranfaglia, that spell out both who the crisis-woman was and the threat she represented:

> A warning has been issued to a Roman newspaper for a drawing showing an excessively thin woman. Given the power of suggestion that such drawings have upon women who are not thin, and the repercussion of forced weight-loss upon fecundity and demographic efficiency, it is best that such drawings no longer be published. (29 July 1932)
>
> È stato fatto un richiamo a un giornale di Roma per un disegno rappresentante una donna eccessivamente magra. Data la suggestione che tali disegni esercitano sulle donne non magre e la ripercussione che i dimagramenti forzati hanno nella prolificità e quindi nelle efficienza demografica, è bene che tali disegni non compaiano più. (29 luglio 1932)[24]
>
> Newspapers have been warned that from this point forward the publication of photographs or figures of thin women will undoubtedly lead to sequestration. (8 February 1933)
>
> È stato avvertito ai giornali che d'ora innanzi la pubblicazione di fotografie o figure di donne magre porterà senz'altro al sequestro. (8 febbraio 1933)[25]
>
> Newspapers have been advised to return to the question of the "crisis-woman" and attempt to circumscribe as much as possible the tendency

that leads women to lose weight and follow exotic fashions, which renders them sterile and unhealthy. (10 February 1933)

È stato raccomandato ai giornali di tornare sulla questione della "donna crisi" cercando di arginare quanto più è possibile la tendenza che porta le donne a dimagrire per seguire mode esotiche, rendendole sterili e malate. (10 febbraio 1933)[26]

Newspapers have been advised to continue to publish photographs of beautiful Italian women and not "crisis" women. (9 March 1933)

È stato raccomandato ai giornali di continuare a pubblicare fotografie di belle donne italiane, non di donne "crisi." (9 marzo 1933)[27]

What I find most interesting about these documents is the manner in which they illustrate the repressive aspects of fascist censorship – namely, restrictions on cultural production – while simultaneously illustrating its positive or productive aspects; although the *veline* purportedly were crafted to ensure the elimination of the *donna-crisi*, they in fact simultaneously encouraged the proliferation of discourse about her (albeit pejorative discourse) and were crucial in securing her meaning as an abject figure in the Italian cultural imagination. From these documents we discover that the exact characteristics of the *donna-crisi* were as follows: she was "unhealthy," "sterile," "masculinized," and "foreign." She was the opposite of the "beautiful Italian" woman, and the "power of suggestion" of this "exotic" figure was so great that the "publication of photographs or figures of thin women" in newspapers and magazines would "lead to sequestration." The defining characteristic of the *donna-crisi*, however, was her "excessive" thinness, taken as visible confirmation of what might otherwise be her indiscernible sterility. It was therefore the duty of the fascist press to eliminate the crisis-woman because she could negatively affect "fecundity and demographic efficiency," which, as Mussolini stressed time and again, was a question of the greatest national importance.

A closer look at representations of the crisis-woman that I describe here and of the modern woman described in the previous section notably does not illustrate the *elimination* of problematic female figures – as the regime asserts in its propaganda – but rather their *control*. [28] Indeed, control is a key concept with regard to the figure of the crisis-woman, and I contend that for the fascist regime there were two primary and interrelated political stakes embodied in discourse about her: control over the changing meaning of the female body and control over the narrative of modernization, which I treat in turn below.

The modern woman and the crisis-woman are two female types sometimes conflated by scholars because they often share an overlapping set of visual signs: knee-length dresses, cropped hair, a trim body, and so on – in short, signs that point to the revolutionary fashion trends of the 1920s. If the modern woman and the crisis-woman were characterized by a frequently overlapping set of signs, then what distinguished them was not simply that one was the product of fascist propaganda and the other was not, but that the cultural value assigned to those signs was different. While the modern woman's short dress might be seen as boldly emancipated, as a symbol of her "brashness" in Brin's terms, the crisis-woman's revealing dress was entirely misguided and ultimately unattractive. While the modern woman focused on "personal satisfaction," the crisis-woman was vain and egotistical. While the modern woman was flirtatiously capricious, the crisis-woman was fickle. While the modern woman was transgressively alluring, the crisis-woman was repulsive. While the modern woman was svelte, the crisis-woman was dangerously thin and sickly.

The overlap between these two figures is significant because it points to the ways in which the *donna-crisi* must necessarily be understood as a figure of control, in particular control over rapidly changing meanings of the female body. The crisis-woman's power to condemn the modern woman and all that she embodied lay precisely in her contiguity with the latter: because of their overlapping iconography, the *donna-crisi* could potentially illuminate the dangers of the modern woman –for example, the dangers of wearing a short dress, wearing pants, or dieting in order to change the shape of the body – through an undesirable taint by association. Otherwise put, the *donna-crisi* was a figure designed to arrest the crisis of signification produced by the multivalence of signs used to represent modern femininity and by extension the female body in the fascist context. Moreover, it is important to note that because the *donna crisi* was portrayed exclusively through verbal description and never through a visual image with an accompanying caption explicitly naming her, she was a figure that could circumscribe the appeal of popular images of the modern woman without becoming enmeshed in the visual codes of desirability that typified them. The sole exception to this defining characteristic is the exaggerated caricatures of the crisis-woman found in satirical newspapers, which I examine in detail in chapter 3. Although visual images of women that may be taken to be crisis-women do exist in many non-satirical publications of the period, this label has invariably been retroactively ascribed by more recent scholars and was never provided by the publications themselves. Such retroactive labelling testifies to the ways in which the *donna-crisi* functioned as an efficacious didactic tool for the promulgation and reinforcement of fascist ideals; indeed, the application of the label *donna-crisi* to various types of modern women was precisely the intent of the figure.

The *donna-crisi* is also a figure that represented the regime's desire to carefully regulate what it meant to be modern. Modernity was a notoriously unstable concept that on the one hand signified positive features like vitality, social progress, economic competitiveness, and the advancement of national interests, but on the other hand evoked ideas of a dangerous internationalism or a threatening urban expansion, and the subsequent need to return to conventional values. The fascist regime was deeply invested in advancing its own version of the modern woman, the *donna nuova,* as the embodiment of the positive terms mentioned above. While the *donna nuova* might have short hair and wear a short skirt, she did so with a sense of moderation and always in the service of health and hygiene. According to fascist logic, she could be easily distinguished from the self-absorbed, individualistic, cosmopolitan modern woman. The May 1928 cover of the philofascist satirical newspaper *420* dramatizes this distinction by showing the *donna nuova* in uniform with her fists raised like a boxer in order to defend herself from a thief, while the modern woman instead cowers weakly in fear (Figure 3).

If through the figure of the *donna nuova,* the regime sought to reappropriate and reframe in positive terms some of the elements that characterized the modern woman, there was also a certain amount of anxiety about the overlapping set of signs they shared. From the 1920s into the 1930s the regime increasingly tried to distinguish the "degenerate" modern woman from her "healthy" modern fascist counterpart, and in the early 1930s the crisis-woman became a type of measuring stick for that distinction: how closely did a woman's choices about her dress and body bring her towards the figure of the *donna-crisi*?

The crisis of multivalence and contradiction that I describe here was a problem not only at the level of sociocultural signification, but also at a structural and political level. Perhaps the most apt vocabulary to describe the gender politics of the Italian context in this moment is that which Victoria de Grazia gives us when she speaks of "the deep conflict

CONTO CORRENTE CON LA POSTA

Anno XIV — N. 702 — Anno VI

FIRENZE, 20 MAGGIO 1928

:: ABBONAMENTI: ::

Italia anno L. 15

Estero ... L. 25

Cent. 30

Per gli avvisi di pubblicità prezzo L. 4 al millimetro giustezza di colonna. — Rivolgersi esclusivamente all'Ufficio E. BAGNINI, Via Vivaio, 10 - MILANO

CASA EDITRICE G. NERBINI

VIA VALFONDA, 21 — FIRENZE

IL 420

" Nodi al pettine "

Articolo di una certa importanza, che riguarda l'attività editoriale e politica dell'*Opera Cardinal Ferrari*.

Solito fervorino che interessa i soliti *certuni* padroni di casa. :: :: ::

« ... io volevo solamente questo: che le donne italiane si abituassero ad essere meno impressionabili, la finissero, cioè, di svenire tutte le volte che vedevano una rivoltella ». (Augusto Turati alle Giovani Italiane).

FINO AD OGGI bastava che un malandrino spianasse una rivoltella di cartone, perchè la donna si spogliasse di borsa e di gioielli... **DOMANI**, la donna educata dal fascismo, se aggredita, saprà difendersi e mettere *knock-out* il suo aggressore.

Figure 3. Cover of the fascist satirical newspaper *420* (May 1928) showing a healthy, modern fascist woman in uniform and a helpless bourgeois modern woman in the pane above her. The caption reads: "Until today, a scoundrel only needed to show a paper revolver to make a woman give up her purse and jewels ... Tomorrow, women educated by fascism, if attacked, will know how to defend themselves and *knock-out* their assailant." (By permission of the Ministero dei beni e delle attività culturali e del turismo della Repubblica Italiana/Biblioteca Nazionale Centrale di Firenze. Reproduction prohibited.)

within the fascist state between the demands of modernity and the desire to re-impose traditional authority" – a conflict that was especially evident in the regime's attitudes towards women.[29] Fascist discourse was continually forced to confront the internal contradiction that in order "to build up national economic strength and to mobilize all of Italian society's resources – including the capacity of women to reproduce and nurture – it inevitably promoted some of the very changes it sought to curb." [30] The multivalence of signs, particularly signs that point to the construction of femininity and modernity, means that we must speak of complex and multiple operations of power in the fascist context. We can't simply assume – and neither does fascist logic assume – the validity of simple equations such as "modern" means "degenerate" and "traditional" means "wholesome" or, on the other hand, "modern" means "subversive" and "traditional" means "hegemonic"; rather, we need to look closely at how fascist power was exercised (and, likewise, resistance was operationalized) in ways that both reinforced and undermined the regime's philosophical and ideological goals and ideals.

The *Donna-crisi* in Women's Magazines

During the years of the campaign against the *donna-crisi,* women's magazines – whether overtly fascist or less political – overwhelmingly characterized the crisis-woman as an abject figure that stood in opposition to the fascist female ideal. Some significant differences among these publications, however, should be noted. Figurations of the crisis-woman in pro-fascist publications are direct, decisive, and often heavy-handed. For example, in July 1933 *Il giornale della donna* summed up this position as follows: "The fascist woman can never be the crisis-woman!! Simply because she knows that her first duty and her greatest pride is that of motherhood" [La donna fascista non potrà mai essere la donna crisi!! Semplicemente perché essa sa, che il suo primo dovere ed il suo più ambito orgoglio è quello di essere madre].[31]

Although tracts decrying the crisis-woman are more numerous in nationalistic magazines such as *Il giornale della donna,* they also appear in more cosmopolitan publications like *Lidel, Amica,* and *Lei.* Allusions to the crisis-woman in these publications, however, often differ in tone: they are more frequently subtle and indirect, but not necessarily less powerful or persuasive.

Take for example an article from *Lidel* that attempts to distinguish between a healthy *snellezza* (slenderness) and an unhealthy *magrezza* (thinness). The editors provide a series of sketches that they say "are our contribution to the … anti-thinness campaign … and serve to demonstrate, we hope in a convincing manner, that there is no incompatibility between today's fashions and a healthy, balanced development of those curves which give a woman's body that soft graciousness which she was proud of for so many centuries" [sono il nostro contributo alla campagna … antidimagrante … e stanno a dimostrare, speriamo in modo convincente, che non v'è incompatibilità fra la moda più recente e un sano ed equilibrato sviluppo di quelle curve che danno al corpo della donna la molle grazie delle quale per tanti secoli è andata fiera].[32] The fact that the editors of *Lidel* chose to argue for the difference between a healthy "slenderness" and an unhealthy "thinness," together with their failure to invoke the crisis-woman directly, might be understood as an attempt to circumvent fascist dictates. But, as my reading of the modern woman shows, scholars need to be aware of the limits of an understanding of primary texts that puts them into oppositional categories of consent and resistance. If we focus instead on the multifaceted operations of power, a much more nuanced reading emerges. Distinguishing between the modern fashion of "slenderness" and an undesirable "thinness" actually dovetails perfectly with the central propagandistic function of the *donna-crisi* – namely, to hold on to a healthy notion of the modern female body by distinguishing between two types of women: in this case, one slender and attractive, one thin and repulsive – that is, one who supported the ideals of the regime and one who undermined them.[33] In short, an ambiguously allusive text such as this one does not necessarily undermine the functioning of the crisis-woman as a regulatory ideal. With her unhealthy thinness she securely remains a figure of policing and control against which women could and should constantly measure themselves.

Perhaps surprisingly, "modern" depictions of women were not the exclusive terrain of more cosmopolitan and less overtly fascist magazines like *Lidel*. Returning to the propagandistic *Il giornale della donna,* we note an interesting column published in May 1933 and titled simply "La moda italiana," which supports the image of women as "both 'modern' and 'traditional'" a conjunction of terms that de Grazia has described as exemplary of fascist propaganda:[34]

> Without returning to the olden days, which would be ridiculous and against the spirit of this century, one can create something "new" which is able wonderfully to blend within it the past that makes up our history, the

> most beautiful history of the world, and which at the same time shapes the imprint of our race.
>
> Senza tornare all'antico che sarebbe ridicolo e contrastante con le esigenze del secolo, si può creare un "nuovo" che sappia mirabilmente fondere in sé quel passato che costituisce la nostra storia, la più bella storia del mondo e che forma nello stesso tempo l'impronta della razza.[35]

The stakes of this "blending" of modern and traditional are extremely high insofar as women's fashion has the ability to "shape the imprint of our race," as the author, Stellina Ronchi, says in a sort of eugenics of style and fashion.

But the tension between modern and traditional that this article raises is soon put to rest. This article is part of a wider referendum on the questions "What is fashion?" and "How might one resolve the problem of creating Italian fashion models?" [Che cos'è la moda? In quale modo si può risolvere il problema di creare dei modelli italiani?] posed by *Il giornale della donna*. Ronchi gives a detailed response to this question that shows exactly what fascist "modern traditionalism" is all about. She argues that "Italian fashion should have its very own illustrations, and in the place of the infamous figure of the crisis-woman it must substitute a florid female figure, that beautiful maternal figure that inspired the poet [Carducci] of a newborn Italy in the 'Canto dell'amore'" [La moda italiana deve avere illustrazioni sue e proprie, dove al famigerato figurino della donna crisi, deve sostituirsi una florida figura muliebre, quella soave figura materna che nel "Canto dell'amore" ispirava il poeta dell'Italia risorta].[36] Ronchi's words are intended to associate the crisis-woman with foreignness and sterility, but her main argument is that fashion is an art, and because Italy has always shown its talent in the field of the arts, it should also succeed in the field of fashion. Italian fashion, she says, should "reflect … the poetry of its land" [riflettere … la poesia della sua terra] and "make more evident the characteristics of our feminine race, that eternal femininity which was so highly celebrated by Carducci, Dante, and Petrarch; that eternal poetry of grace and sentiment which Rafael and Perugino knew how to depict so well in their Madonnas" [far meglio risaltare le caratteristiche della nostra razza femminile, quell'eterno femminino che fu così altamente celebrato dal Carducci, da Dante e dal Petrarca; quell'eterna poesia di grazia e di sentimento che Rafaello e Perugino seppero così ben ritrarre nelle loro Madonne].[37] Ronchi concludes that "Italian fashion will know how to give back to our women every breath of grace and poetry by returning most of all ... to that *Naturalness* which provided the ideal of female beauty to our great artists" [La moda italiana saprà ridonare alla nostra donna ogni soffio di grazia e di poesia ritornando soprattutto ... a quella *Naturalezza* che fornò l'ideale femminile dei nostri grandi].[38] As we have seen, during the 1930s fashion became a key battleground for defining and controlling not simply a new style but women and women's bodies. Here Ronchi legitimates the maternal body as both the natural body and the national body standing against the artificiality and foreignness of the crisis-woman's body. Art and nature close in upon themselves in a neat tautological formula: artists from Dante to Rafael to Carducci have "celebrated" the maternal "characteristics of our feminine race" at the same time that these characteristics inspired artists and "provided" them with an "ideal of female beauty." Italian art celebrates women's nature, which in turn inspires Italian art. Thus Italian fashion, because it is nothing less than Italian art, must also celebrate and be inspired by the natural female body, which, of course, is synonymous with the maternal body.

More cosmopolitan magazines and less overtly fascist women's magazines, interestingly enough, also sometimes contained less subtle articles on thinness that seemed copied straight from the pages of the *veline*. A good example is the article "Le grasse e le magre" ["Chubby and Thin Women"] published in *Amica* in November 1932. With the common gesture of linking fashion to eugenics, the author Valentino Piccoli argues that "the problem of fat and thin women" [il problema delle grasse e le magre] can no longer have "the tone of a frivolous discussion" [il tono di una frivola discussione] because the way in which women shape their figure directly influences the well-being of the Italian people as a whole: "Aesthetics," he says "is closely connected to the health, strength, and efficiency of the race" [L'estetica si collega strettamente alla salute, alla forza, all'efficienza della razza].[39] Given his eugenicist understanding of "aesthetics" – or, in other words, fashion – it is not surprising that Piccoli's view of women is perfectly in line with hegemonic fascist ideals: "One of the greatest moral forces of fascist civilization lies exactly in woman's perennial call to her noblest mission as spiritual guide (to human life) and as mother, as sweet benefactor and efficient force in the life of the people" [Una delle più grandi forze morali della civiltà fascista è appunto in questo perenne richiamo della donna alle sue più nobili missioni di animatrice (alla vita umana) e di madre, di benefattrice soave e di forza efficiente nella vita dei popoli].[40] In his view, the fascist vision of woman is correct because it follows the rules of nature whereas the thin woman – an indirect but unmistakable allusion to the *donna-crisi* – embodies a type of deleterious unnatural femininity: "The trend of 'watching one's waist' has lead, and still leads, some women to follow dieting regimes which are destructive to their health. With these regimes, women go against nature and damage themselves and their progeny" [La moda di "conservare la linea" ha condotto e conduce talora alcune signore a fare delle cure dimagranti che sono deleterie alla salute. Con queste cure, la donna va contro la natura e danneggia sé stessa e la sua progenie].[41]

The most chilling argument that Piccoli makes is that "watching one's waist" is in fact a criminal act: "Those who damage themselves commit a crime against others; and a crime is committed most of all by the woman who, for false vanity, for frivolous and blind adhesion to fashions which come from across the Alps, does not hesitate to ruin her own health and ready herself to give birth to weak, sick children who are condemned to suffer the consequences of sterile maternal vanity" [Chi danneggia sé stesso, compie un delitto contro gli altri; e sopra tutto lo compie una donna che, per falsa vanità, per frivola e supina adesione alle mode d'oltralpe, non esita a rovinare la propria salute e a prepararsi a generare figli deboli, malaticci, condannati a subire le conseguenze della sterile vanità materna].[42] The woman who thins herself according to foreign fashions is thus merely succumbing to vanity, which is both "false" and "sterile" even in mothers. Piccoli's invocation of the juridical realm suggests Foucault's idea in *Discipline and Punish* that the "law is not literally internalized, but incorporated, with the consequence that bodies are produced which signify that law on and through the body … the law is at once fully manifest and fully latent, for it never appears as external to the bodies it subjects and subjectivates."[43] In short, for Piccoli, both the body of the *donna-madre* and that of the *donna-crisi* are not only governed by but also shaped by fascist law. The difference between the two is simply that the first lies within the domain of cultural intelligibility while the second lies outside it. That Piccoli's description of the thin woman adheres so completely to fascist ideological dictates, even though it is published in a rather cosmopolitan magazine, shows us just how pervasive and common such notions of femininity were.

As I have shown in this chapter, from the start of the twentieth century fashion was a rapidly evolving, politically and ideologically charged discourse that especially highlighted new ideas about gender, sex, and the female body. In the mid-1920s classic twenties style put into question the core values and precepts – embodied in the maternal and domestic ideal – that the newly founded fascist regime was working to establish. At this time, women's fashion magazines often depicted the female body as a liminal space where social and ideological struggles were played out. Although these complex depictions were frequently circumscribed in their potential to undermine the category of the natural body upon which the fascist subject was grounded, they were nevertheless quite powerful. As I will show in the following chapter, as fascist institutions and policies became established, the discourse of fashion became increasingly aligned with the social sciences and turned its attention to a regulation of the borders of the natural female body. In the chapters that follow we will explore this policing in scientific, satirical, and political discourse, but we will also ask if the abject can turn into a figure of resistance for those who opposed the regime's ideals.

2

Scientific Discourse and the Making of the Donna-crisi

Among the various popular trends of the 1930s described by Irene Brin – the lively writer and journalist whom we encountered at the start of chapter 1 – was the so-called hygiene trend. In her distinctive, witty idiom, Brin writes of the transnational craze for fresh air, body treatments, exercise, and dieting: "Incredible words came out of the mouths of senators who were, at one time, epicureans and *bon vivants*: 'My cold shower, my push-ups, my fruit-day.' Vigorously pounding their chests, everyone confirmed that they felt more youthful" [Parole incredibili uscivano dalle labbra di senatori un tempo buongustai e ben viventi: "La mia doccia fredda, le mie flessioni, il mio giorno-di-frutta." Battendosi vigorosamente il petto, tutti assicuravano di sentirsi ringiovaniti].[1] Brin writes that as a result of the hygiene trend "there was not only the soul but the body to be cured" [Non c'era solo l'anima da curare, ma il corpo].[2] Her description of Italy's hygiene mania points to the intimate connection between health and beauty in the fascist state, and the implicit imperative for all citizens to embody both.

The connection between health and beauty is a longstanding one that, as Sander Gilman points out in *Picturing Health and Illness*, "acquired its most explicit statement at the close of the nineteenth century."[3] Gilman specifies that "it is not only that the healthy becomes the beautiful, but that the beautiful becomes the healthy; the diseased is not only the ugly, but the ugly the diseased."[4] Indeed, Brin's description of fascist Italy's hygiene mania perfectly illustrates the thinly veiled fear that beauty's malevolent counterpart, ugliness or disease, lurked right around the corner and must be vigilantly kept at bay. Gilman concludes by specifically underscoring the role of science in this equation: "the ugly must be made to give way to the beautiful though the agency of *scientific medicine.*"[5] This was especially true for a cultural phenomenon like the hygiene trend, in which fashion and science operated in tandem: fashion occupied itself with cultivating and maintaining beauty while science attempted to contain or cure the pathological, the deviant, the ugly, and the diseased.

This chapter, which focuses on representations of the crisis woman in scientific discourse, is structured as a complement to the preceding chapter on fashion. Although the crisis-woman appears less frequently in scientific discourse than in fashion texts, understanding her place in the former is crucial to understanding it within the latter, since scientific ways of examining, knowing, and constituting the body permeate the world of fashion precisely, as Gilman puts it, in order to enable the ugly "to give way to the beautiful." In the pages that follow I show how specialized scientific discourse profoundly influences popular and more widespread depictions of the crisis-woman and illustrate the ways in which the pathological body of the crisis-woman is not simply an object of scrutiny or a disparaged figure under the regime, but in fact a useful *construction* and *product* of fascist science in service of some of the regime's most important ideals and goals.

The Crisis-Woman and Nicola Pende's Political Biology

Nicola Pende was a politically well-connected doctor who began his distinguished career in 1903 and led an active professional life under the regime: he headed the medical clinic of the University of Genoa, was named director of the planned but unrealized government agency Istituto di bonifica umana ed ortogenesi della razza [Institute of Human Improvement and Racial Orthogenesis], was named a senator by Mussolini, and was among the most prominent of the signatories of the infamous 1938 "Manifesto degli scienziati razzisti" [Manifesto of Racist Scientists], which was published in the newspaper *Il popolo d'Italia* a few months before the racial laws took effect.[6] Internationally recognized for his research in endocrinology, Pende is perhaps best known for his writings on the science of constitutionalism, or the study of how one's physical constitution (or in Pende's words, one's "biotype") is a direct indicator of one's overall health.[7] Like his famed predecessor Cesare Lombroso, Pende viewed the body as a privileged site for making deviance legible, and he interpreted constitutional defects as a sign of imminent danger to the individual as well as to society.[8] Again like Lombroso, he was deeply interested in the improvement of the Italian nation through racial enhancement.[9] As Carl Ipsen writes, Pende "believed that by monitoring individual growth anthropometrically, pathologically, socially, etc. one could adjust environment and nutrition to ensure individual and ultimately racial improvement."[10] Finally, Pende did not just carry out medical research to realize this goal; he also advocated for numerous social changes such as the institution of personal eugenic record-books (the *libretto individuale biotipologico-sanitario*) in primary and secondary schools, as well as obligatory health certificates for couples that wished to marry.[11]

As far as the *donna-crisi* is concerned, what is particularly significant about Pende's research is the manner in which it dovetails with the fascist political and ideological agenda – particularly that surrounding the demographic campaign. Indeed, as Ipsen confirms, "The studies conducted by 'constitutional' scientists (Pende included) on the presumed relationship between fertility and biotypes were often brought up in the context of the demographic campaign."[12] Pende's contribution to the International Conference on Demography, hosted in Rome in 1931 at the height of the crusade against the crisis-woman, is an excellent example of this type of political scientific writing. His paper, entitled "Costituzione e fecondità" ["Constitution and Fecundity"], discusses the loaded topic of the physical characteristics of prolific women. Pende presents the findings of his experiment comparing two anthropomorphic measurements in adult women: the distance between the shoulders and the distance between the hips, or, in the medical terminology of the day, the bisacromial measurement (the measurement between the two acromial processes of the shoulders) and the bitrochanteric measurement (the measurement between the greater trochanters of each femur). The findings of his study can be reduced to one relatively simple conclusion: the fertile "maternal type" of woman, as Pende calls her, has hips that are broader than her shoulders while the less fertile "non-maternal type" has broader shoulders and narrower hips – in other words, an anatomy associated with male bodies. Pende explains:

> It is very evident that the maternal woman is distinguished from the non-maternal by an excess of the bitrochanteric diameter with regard to the median female bitrochanteric measurement (32.2 [centimetres] as compared to 31.4), and by a deficiency in the bisacromial measurement (30.8 as compared to 31.2), while in the non-maternal woman the bisacromial measurement is at least as great as the median and the bitrochanteric is less – in other words, one finds the opposite configuration.

> È evidentissimo che la donna madre si distingue dalla non madre per un eccesso di diametro bitrocanterico, di fronte al bitrocanterico medio femminile (32,2 di fronte a 31,4) e per un difetto del bisacromiale (30,8 di fronte a 31,2): mentre nella donna non madre il bisacromiale è alquanto maggiore della media ed il bitrocanterico è minore, in altri termini si ha il comportamento opposto.[13]

Pende supplements these findings with an analysis of what were understood to be secondary "sexual" characteristics – such as endocrine make-up, a personal history of menstruation and menopause, and a count of births and abortions – all of which confirm his original thesis.

What interests me here is the manner in which Pende's study, like much fascist science, is as unabashedly ideological as it is scientific. Pende maps the contours of two "biotypes": "the interesting fact found by me and confirmed by my [female] students Gualco and Sarperi is that there exists, from the point of view of the general sexual shape of the body, and precisely from the point of view of the relation between the upper and lower breadth of the body, a *maternal* and *non-maternal type* of woman" [Ma il fatto interessante trovato da me e confermato dalle mie allieve Gualco e Sarperi è che esiste, dal punto di vista della linea generale sessuale del corpo, e precisamente dal punto di vista del rapporto tra larghezza superiore e larghezza inferiore, un *tipo non materno* ed un *tipo materno* di donna.][14] These biological, medical types neatly correspond to two readily identifiable and politically charged cultural types that Italians of the 1930s would know very well: the *donna-madre* and the *donna-crisi*. The politics driving Pende's science could not be more clear: his study reinforces the cultural norm of the robust prolific female body type that was heralded by the regime while condemning its opposite.

On this same note, Pende likens deviance from the maternal biotype to sexual deviance: "In *eunuchs* we find that the breadth of the shoulders diminishes together with that of the torso while the breadth of the pelvis and thighs increases; the opposite is true in many *inter-sexual* and *virile women* where we find a masculine line in the torso, broad at the top and narrow below" [Negli uomini *eunucoidi* noi troviamo che la larghezza delle spalle diminuisce e così quella del torace, e cresce la larghezza del bacino e delle cosce e viceversa in molte donne *intersessuali* e *viriloidi* troviamo la linea maschile del tronco, larga in alto e stretta in basso].[15] With no particular empirical grounding, Pende goes on to link the crucial measurement that distinguishes the maternal from the non-maternal woman with evolutionary and racial advancement as well as civilization itself: "the more one progresses evolutionarily, from the savage woman to the woman of the civilized races, the more pronounced this greater width of the pelvis becomes when compared to that of the shoulders" [più si sale nell'evoluzione dalla donna selvaggia alla donna delle razze civilizzate e più questa larghezza maggiore della pelvi di fronte alla larghezza delle spalle si accentua].[16] As Pende's other writings show, he views body shape not simply as the luck of the draw but as something that must be unceasingly managed and carefully controlled by the fascist state. In short, for Pende – and we might say more generally for fascist ideologues – the shape of one's body necessarily had a moral, ethical, social, and political dimension.

Pende's propensity to classify the body into distinct types was typical of the period and demonstrates the reach and influence of positivist science. The discerning reader cannot help but wonder if a centimetre's difference between the average hip and shoulder measurements of the maternal and non-maternal woman – scarcely discernable to the naked eye – could really indicate such a radical biological, sexual, moral, and developmental difference between two human beings; nevertheless such typologies carried considerable weight not only with scientists like Pende but with journalists, writers, and more broadly those engaged with the cultural dissemination of ideas in Italy in these years.[17]

In 1933, two years after the International Conference on Demography and the publication of his "Costituzione e fecondità," Pende published a major work entitled *Bonifica umana razionale e biologia politica* [*Rationalistic Human Improvement and Political Biology*]. In this book, he coins the term "political biology" – that is, biological research designed to inform political policy – and makes this the focal point of his text.[18] He explains that while the scientist in the fascist state engages in *political biology*, the statesman engages in its complementary opposite, *biological politics*. Naturally, the tome is dedicated "To Benito Mussolini, who with sound principles of biological politics has woven a physical, moral, and intellectual new suit for a great, new Country" [A Benito Mussolini che con i principî sani della politica biologica tesse un abito fisico, morale ed intellettuale nuovo per una nuova grande Patria].[19] These mutually beneficial projects of the scientist and the statesman anticipate, in certain ways, what Foucault would later call biopolitics, or the self-interested concern of the state for the biological well-being of its citizens. But while Foucault evidences the operations of power and the construction of knowledge in the service of social control, Pende conceals the former and valorizes the latter.

Throughout *Bonifica umana*, women, and the countless "problems" associated with them, are among Pende's central targets for "human improvement."[20] Like many researchers of his day, Pende viewed the active role women played in the declining birth rate as one of the nation's most serious concerns.[21] On this topic, he writes:

> The problem of the decline in birth rates, or hyponatalism – a problem that the Head of the Government, with his eagle eye, immediately identified as the most vital problem for the development of the Nation – is not one of those problems that can be light-heartedly taken on and discussed by whomever – whether expert or dilettante – is interested in sociological phenomena; this is because we are speaking of a problem that is, first of all, biological and medical.
>
> Il problema della diminuzione delle nascite, od iponatalità, problema che il Capo del Governo, col suo occhio d'aquila, ha presto segnalato come il problema più vitale per l'avvenire della Nazione, non è di quelli che possono a cuor leggero essere affrontati e discussi da chiunque si interessi, da competente a dilettante, di fenomeni sociologici, e ciò perché si tratta di un problema innanzi tutto biologico e medico.[22]

Then, speaking from a medical point of view, Pende proceeds to delineate a series of interlaced social problems in which women play a key role.

For Pende, addressing the threatening decline in birth rates involves, first and foremost, banning the phenomenon of the working mother. He categorically condemns the "deleterious influence that work – both manual and intellectual – combined with the tiring functions of gestation and lactation, has upon the organism of the mother and that of the children" [influenza deleteria che il lavoro sia manuale che intellettuale, combinato con le faticose funzioni della gestazione e dell'allattamento, esercita così sull'organismo della madre che su quello dei figli].[23] To underscore his point, he refers to a "common-sense" observation, drawn from the natural world: "the female mother ... does not work in any zoological species" [la femmina madre ... non lavora in nessuna specie zoologica].[24] Tellingly, Pende redundantly refers to the "*female* mother" – a wording that reveals just how close he is to arguing that work is dangerous not only to mothers but to females as a whole. He goes on to criticize women's participation in sports, especially those that in his opinion should be reserved for men: "the woman who, equal to a man, cultivates certain sports ... ends up insensibly affected by damage to the psychic and somatic sphere of her sexuality" [la donna che coltiva al pari dell'uomo, certi sport ... finisce col risentire insensibilmente un danno nella sfera somatica e psichica della sua sessualità].[25] Finally, he turns his attention to the fashion of thinning down, which he feels encourages women "to keep one's figure eternally adolescent" in the name of beauty:

> But the modern cult of the "maschietta," as Spengler says, trains the body of woman not for the functions of maternity, but for the excesses of sport; it acts, above all, psychologically, making the sacred sentiment of maternity take second place to the need to keep one's figure eternally adolescent, and to the belief – false from a biological point of view – that the *donna madre* soils her beauty and her robustness earlier than the woman who avoids procreation and the sacrifices imposed by the functions of maternity."

> Ma il culto moderno della "maschietta," che come dice Spengler, educa il corpo della donna non per le funzioni di maternità, ma per gli eccessi sportivi, agisce soprattutto in senso psicologico, facendo passare in seconda linea nella mentalità della donna il sacro sentimento della maternità di fronte al bisogno di conservare eternamente adolescente la linea del proprio corpo, di fronte alla credenza, falsa dal punto di vista biologico, che la donna madre logori la propria bellezza e la propria robustezza più precocemente che la donna la quale eviti la procreazione ed i sacrifici che impongono le funzioni della maternità.[26]

Pende's lament soon reaches a fever pitch: "Not having children, or having only one at the most, in order to maintain an elegant figure, in order to avoid gaining the weight evidenced by gestation and lactation, in order not to age too quickly!" [Non fare figli, o farne uno solo al massimo, per conservare la linea elegante, per evitare l'ingrassamento che può verificarsi per le gestazioni e gli allattamenti, per non invecchiare troppo presto!].[27] For him, the idea is preposterous.

Pende's medical preoccupation with social phenomena such as work, sports, or fashion shows just how thoroughly, by the 1930s, these spheres are intertwined. As Nikolas Rose puts it: "Medicine ... has played a formative role in the *invention of the social*."[28] That is to say, "it has been bound up with the ways in which ... the very idea of *society* has been brought into existence and acquired a density and a form."[29] Rose goes on to give a description of society that is particularly apt for fascist society as Pende conceives of it: "Society, as it is historically invented, is immediately accorded an organic form and thought in medical terms. As a *social body* it is liable to sickness: that is to say it is problematized in the vocabulary of medicine. As a social body it needs to be restored to health: that is to say, its government is conceptualized in medical terms."[30] Although in his writing on demographic decline Pende never explicitly alludes to the crisis-woman – a figure who represented a grave and imminent threat to the social body – his dual concepts of political biology and biological politics together with his foundational work on maternal and non-maternal biotypes clearly form the scientific background for other, more popular condemnations of the *donna-crisi*, to which I turn shortly.

Before moving on, however, I should observe that like many authors who write about the crisis-woman, Pende makes general and specific calls for the government to take action. Using the military language that characterizes the demographic campaign, he argues that "the state ... must intervene with all possible weapons so that Italian women, too, understand national necessities" [lo stato ... deve con ogni sua arma intervenire perché anche la donna in Italia comprenda le necessità nazionali].[31] He goes on: "It is necessary that our Government not only protect mothers and children, *but prepare future mothers*" [È necessario che il nostro Governo non solo protegga la madre e il bambino, *ma prepari le future madri*].[32] Such preparation would involve "new laws and new institutions that concern themselves, a bit more than has been the case until now, with the woman question" [nuove leggi e nuove istituzioni che si occupino, un po' più che finora non sia stato fatto, del problema femminile].[33] Pende calls upon the government to take firmer control of primary and secondary education for girls: "From early childhood, we need to oversee the formation of the Italian woman, with fascistic knowledge, with a new educative direction – obligatory in primary and secondary schools – that aims to form housewives and the *donna madre*" [Occorre con sapienza fascistica dirigere la formazione della donna italiana, fino dalla prima fanciullezza, con un nuovo indirizzo educativo, obbligatorio nelle scuole primarie e secondarie, che miri a formare il tipo della donna di casa e della donna madre].[34] This educational initiative would also involve "a sexual educative direction that continually instills in the naive and inexpert mind of the young girl the concept of the true significance of the somatic and psychic attributes of her sex, attributes all destined by nature for the maternal function" [un indirizzo educativo sessuale che istilli diuturnamente nell'anima ingenua ed inesperta della giovinetta il concetto del vero significato che hanno gli attributi somatici e psichici del suo sesso, attributi tutti destinati dalla natura alla funzione materna].[35] Not just girls but young women and women who are already mothers would come under stricter control: "The State also needs to limit, as much as possible, women's work outside of the home, and perhaps impede altogether work by pregnant and nursing mothers, or those that have children to care for who are less than two years old" [Occorre inoltre che lo Stato limiti al minimo possibile il lavoro delle donne fuori della loro casa; e impedisca forse del tutto il lavoro delle gestanti e delle madri che allattano, o che hanno bambini da accudire, inferiori a due anni].[36] Finally, economically disadvantaged women would come under the "protection" of the state, although not for entirely altruistic reasons: "The State and public welfare, lastly, need to encourage the marriage of poor young women who, out of misery, remain single and are constrained to compete with men for positions in workshops and offices" [Occorre infine che lo Stato e la beneficenza pubblica incoraggino con le borse di meritaggio il matrimonio delle fanciulle povere, che per miseria rimangono nubili e sono costrette a contendere all'uomo i posti nelle officine e negli uffici].[37]

Pende uses his biological research to address a larger and perhaps more vexing philosophical question: how do we define "woman" in a modern day and age? For him, the essence of woman lies in her ability to reproduce: "Hegel, the illustrious German sociologist, said 'He who is not a father, is not a man,' but perhaps more correctly (and we hope more efficaciously) we can say 'she who does not want to know how to be a mother, does not merit the very noble title of woman, that is, of a lady and a queen of man and the family'" [Egel, il sociologo tedesco illustre, ha detto: "Non è uomo chi non è padre" ma forse con maggior ragione (speriamo anche con maggior efficacia) noi potremmo dire: "non merita il titolo nobilissimo di donna, cioè di signora e regina dell'uomo e della famiglia, chi non vuole o non sa essere madre"].[38] And, as he says elsewhere: "Either woman is physically and mentally adapted to being the wife of man and a mother, or she is not truly a woman" [O la donna è conformata fisicamente e mentalmente per essere sposa dell'uomo e madre, o non è veramente donna].[39]

But all of this scientific and social theory does not tie up into a neat philosophical package. There is a distinct sense throughout Pende's writings that women and their bodies are not as pliable as he would like, and that they actively resist the type of shaping he proposes. Take, for example, the following passage:

in the final analysis ... the task of stopping the continued deterioration of the social malady of the decline of births, leading as [Richard] Korherr and Benito Mussolini have justly proclaimed to the death of the nations, ... *lies essentially with the modern woman. If women want*, if they stop deserting the domestic nest to compete with man in the workplace or in sporting pleasures, if they renounce – most of all – the pernicious superstition that procreation is damaging to the aesthetic of their own body, the evil of hyponatalism shall be defeated in the course of a few years.

è ... *essenzialmente alla donna moderna che spetta*, in ultima analisi ... il compito di impedire che la malattia sociale del decremento delle nascite continui ad aggravarsi, conducendo come Korherr e Benito Mussolini hanno altamente proclamato, alla morte dei popoli. *Se le donne vorranno*, se esse rinunzieranno a disertare il nido domestico per concorrere con l'uomo nel lavoro o nei piaceri sportivi, se rinunzieranno soprattutto alla perniciosa superstizione che il procreare sia dannoso all'estetica del proprio corpo, il male dell'iponatalità sarà in poco volgere d'anni debellato.[40]

The power to change Italy's destiny tellingly lies in the hands of women, and in particular *modern* women – not men – in this passage. Perhaps this is why Pende states that he believes the "female problem" [problema femminile] is "in large part subordinate to the so-called demographic problem" [in massima parte subordinato al cosiddetto problema demografico].[41] Noticeably, the threat of women's growing autonomy underpins much of Pende's biopolitics. His anxieties are even more relevant if one takes into consideration oral historical accounts, such as that evidenced in the work of Elizabeth Kraus and Luisa Passerini, which suggest that women's resistance to fascist demographic policy – especially in the practices of *coitus interruptus* and home abortions – was particularly strong and varied.[42] Pende's writing, in the final analysis, attests not only to a disciplinary fantasy and to the will to control women's bodies, but also, significantly, to the ways in which that fantasy was constantly thwarted by women's very real and undeniable desire to change their traditional roles in fascist society.

The Semiotics of the Crisis-Woman in Popular Scientific Writing

It may be surprising to find, as we turn to less specialized scientific writings, that the "low culture" of fashion was of significant interest to the "high culture" of the medical world. Articles on women's fashions crop up in a wide variety of places, from conference proceedings to advice columns in specialized publications. Here I will examine several articles published in the socio-scientific journal *Maternità ed infanzia* [*Maternity and Infancy*], which was the principle publication of the ONMI and effectively functioned as a forum for disseminating the regime's demographic and social welfare policies, particularly with regard to women. The publication was a venue for articles – most often written by doctors and scientists – on a wide range of topics such as nursing and lactation practices, the latest pediatric research, or the infant morality rate in various hospitals. Many of these writings are characterized by technical language and specialized information, but – keeping true to its edifying and educational goals – *Maternità ed infanzia* also published editorials that were accessible to the general public and most often targeted women.

The March 1933 article "Aberrazioni moderne: La linea" ["Modern Aberrations: The Figure"] provides an excellent example of this vulgate genre. Written in an engaging, extremely readable style and completely void of scholarly references or technical terms, this article expresses grave concerns about the fashionable trend of thinning down. Although the *donna-crisi* is not explicitly mentioned, she is clearly the unnamed figure behind the author's condemnation of the "modern aberration" of the slender female form. Take, for example, the following description of young women who, believing themselves to be smart and stylish, end up as skinny and unhealthy as the crisis-woman: "Nourished by a bit of cooked greens, coffee, and tea – all of which is dressed with the abundant smoke of cigarettes – they become thin as toothpicks" [Nutrite d'un po' d'erba cotta, di caffé, di thè, il tutto condito dall'abbondante fumo delle sigarette, si riducono magre come stuzzicadenti].[43] The author, identified only by the not-so-subtly fascio-religious pen name "Fiducia," criticizes the obsession with the "thin as toothpicks" female figure as a particularly outmoded trend: in her opinion, the "modern aberration" of slimming down is paradoxically an aberration precisely because it is not modern. Linking the trend of watching one's waist to the restrictive fashions of the nineteenth century, Fiducia's logic is as follows: if the corset was "the tyrant of the beauties of the past" [il tiranno delle belle d'allora], then "the *figure* has become the tyrant of our young girls" [La *linea* è divenuta la tiranna delle nostre fanciulle].[44] The havoc this contemporary tyrant wreaks on the bodies of "our" (i.e., not only Italian but fascist) young girls is self-evident: "Each one of us knows the damage produced by the so-called thinning cures" [Ognuno di noi sa i danni prodotti dalle così dette cure dimagranti].[45] Unsurprisingly, Fiducia toes the fascist party line and argues that women's reproductive functions suffer the most from this retrograde trend: "Malnourished and graceful organisms will never be able to produce strong offspring, thus making useless the sacrifices that the Country has sustained in order to protect children, to heal them, and to favour in every way the physical life of adolescence and youth" [Organismi denutriti e gracili non potranno mai procreare una forte prole; e diverranno inutili allora i sacrifici che la Patria sopporta per proteggere i bambini, per curarli, per favorire in ogni modo la vita fisica dell'adolescenza e della gioventù].[46] Obliquely referring to the regime's welfare policies ("the sacrifices that the Country has sustained in order to protect children"), Fiducia supports the traditional fascist argument that women's bodies are most valuable for their reproductive capabilities. In short, as for Pende, a woman is by definition a mother. In the end, the "aberration" that Fiducia speaks of is not only a paradoxically outmoded fashion trend but also a throwback body type: the decadent "malnourished and graceful" but ultimately weak body, the abnormally thin body, the anti-maternal body, in short, the body of the crisis-woman.

In 1934, in an article entitled simply "Donna 'Crisi'," doctor Camilla Nervi moves the crisis-woman from backstage to centre stage in the pages of *Maternità ed Infanzia*.[47] Nervi's piece is notable for its vituperative tone and for the fact that it condenses a wide variety of tropes about the *donna-crisi*: she associates the crisis-woman with physical and moral degeneration; she speaks of her bodily deformation; she takes for granted her sexual promiscuity; she links the crisis-woman to disease; and she suggests that the crisis-woman contributes to the decline of the race. Before I embark on an analysis of these tropes, however, it is useful to consider the ways in which this text calls upon the reader to recognize, or read, the signs of the deviant body of the *donna-crisi*.

Nervi opens her article with the assertion that she will explain the birth of the crisis-woman: "Let us examine the origin of the phenomenon: we see how, all of a sudden, society realized that too many women had become rather too thin: all equal figures, equally slender and stylized, coming a bit too close to the masculine body type" [Esaminiamo la genesi del fenomeno: troviamo come ad un tratto la società si fosse accorta che troppe donne erano divenute di dimensioni assai ridotte: figure tutte eguali, tutte egualmente sottili e stilizzate, avvicinatesi un po' troppo al tipo morfologico mascolino].[48] Notably, as soon as Nervi identifies the deviance of the crisis-woman's body – a body whose thinness represents the deadening homogeneity of modernity ("equally slender and stylized") as well as its dangerous blurring of gender lines ("coming a bit too close to the masculine body type") – her discussion shifts away from considering the origins of the "phenomenon" and takes on the tone of a medical examination. In addition to the crisis-woman's irregular thinness, Nervi notes her "caved-in cheeks" [guance smunte], her "anemic eyes" [occhi anemici], and the "false floridness" [finta floridezza] of her complexion, which can only be partially hidden with makeup.[49] "Looking at a "crisis" girl," she says, "I remember often feeling as I felt during visits to a sanatorium" [Ricordo di aver provato spesso, guardando una ragazza "crisi" la stessa impressione che provai in un sanatorio].[50] In this opening paragraph, what Nervi ends up showing her reader is not so much the origins of the phenomenon of the crisis-woman as the signs by which one might identify her: a body that is too thin, a haggard face, and a pale complexion. Like the majority of commentators who write about the *donna-crisi*, Nervi assumes that the signs of the crisis-woman's deviance are manifest, above all, in her body. Moreover, as a doctor, Nervi is in a privileged position to decode this deviant body, making it recognizable to the lay reader and thus fulfilling what fascism would call her "prophylactic" duty to protect the individual as well as the social body from disease.

The notion, first, that the body is a privileged site for making deviance legible, and second, that the physician is uniquely positioned to identify this deviance, originates most immediately in medical practice of the late nineteenth century.[51] Perhaps of greatest influence on popular writers like Nervi and technical writers like Pende was the work of Cesare Lombroso, a doctor, professor of forensic medicine, professor of hygiene, psychiatrist, and positivist criminal anthropologist. In his work, Lombroso attempted to establish a clear relationship between deviant bodies and deviant behaviour, and he viewed aberrant physical features as a sign of grave social danger. With the ultimate goal of reducing and even preventing crime, he meticulously taxonomized the bodies of imprisoned criminals in order to establish their distinguishing traits. Thick eyebrows, a heavy-set jaw, or deviation from the average skull shape could all be the marks – or as Lombroso called them, the "stigmata" – of the almost subhuman species known as "criminal man" and "criminal woman."

In order to make deviance legible, and by implication containable, Lombroso employed the techniques of what was then cutting-edge empirical scientific research. This involved the extremely detailed measurement of body parts and facial features with the aid of modern devices such as an Anfosso tachianthropometer to measure anatomical proportions or a Zwaardesmaker olfactometer to measure sense of smell. Lombroso and his colleagues generated detailed scientific information that not only made the deviant body an object of scientific study, but discursively constructed it in completely new ways.[52] Thanks to Lombroso's work, scientists, politicians, legislators, and ostensibly even the average person could identify different criminal types – the "born criminal," the "insane criminal," the "occasional criminal," and others – each of whom had a unique set of physical and psychological characteristics. In short, Lombroso not only proposed an innovative and profoundly influential medical approach to identifying deviance through somatic signs, but also proposed what might be considered a new and highly influential positivist semiotics of the body. Drawing on Lombroso's legacy, Camilla Nervi identifies the characteristics of another deviant type: the *donna-crisi*.

David Horn has proposed an especially productive approach to teasing out the larger cultural legacy of Lombroso's scientific writing, especially given the fact that the somatic differences in "body types" he identifies were most often contradictory or so negligible as to be statistically insignificant and certainly indistinguishable to the naked eye.[53] Horn argues that "the anthropometrical data" – excruciatingly meticulous measurements of the body that were graphically organized into easily readable yet technical charts – "produced in the pages of *L'uomo delinquente* are, if nothing else, traces of an obsessive poring over the criminal body."[54] This "obsessive poring," which is at the heart of nearly all of Lombroso's writing (and likewise crucial to Nervi's classification), can be more fully understood when it is linked to Foucault's notion of the clinical gaze, that is, the probing gaze of the physician that seeks to identify the pathology of the human body.

Foucault argues in *The Birth of the Clinic* that the revolutionary reorganization of the medical profession in the eighteenth century fundamentally changed the operations of power in this field. As medical historian Thomas Osborne explains, "Foucault associates the clinical revolution of the eighteenth century with the convergence of new forms of observation of patients (associated with hospital structures, in situ education, etc.)."[55] These "new forms of observation" crystallize in the clinical gaze, which concentrates power in the penetrating eye of the institutionally sanctioned doctor as it decodes the signs of the ailing patient's body. As Foucault writes, only the "careful gaze" of the physician "has the power to bring a truth to light."[56] Only this gaze can make the ailing body speak, and it is via this gaze that the pathological body of the individual, rather than more generalized disease, becomes the object and product of modern medical knowledge.[57]

One of the most significant aspects of Foucault's writing is the notion that the pathological body is a *product* of modern medicine as much as it is an *object* of scrutiny – an observation that we might also apply to the figure of the crisis-woman. As medical sociologist David Armstrong says: "the reality of the body is only established by the observing eye that reads it."[58] To illustrate his point, Armstrong gives the example of the anatomical atlas – a book that provides a visual map for the different systems of the body (muscular, reproductive, digestive, etc.). He argues that the atlas "enables the anatomy student, when faced with the undifferentiated amorphous mass of the body, to see certain things and ignore others. In effect, what the student sees is not the atlas as a representation of the body but the body as a representation of the atlas."[59] Armstrong's point is that the clinical gaze, in effect, is an apparatus of power that creates the body insofar as it makes an "undifferentiated mass" legible and knowable. Lombroso's writing, with its "obsessive poring" over the criminal body, has the same function as the atlas – it works to construct the deviant body at the same time that it decodes it.

If we return to Nervi's article describing the telltale symptoms of the *donna-crisi* – "caved-in cheeks," "anemic eyes" and "false floridness" – we can see that her suggestive analogy, which links the crisis-woman to the tubercular patient convalescing in a sanatorium, puts us squarely in the territory of the clinic. One might also argue that insofar as Nervi maps out a medicalized gaze that penetrates and decodes the pathological female body, she also unwittingly performatively enacts the creation of the crisis-woman. Like the anatomical atlas, she enables the lay reader to map the contours of the body of the crisis-woman. Moreover, Nervi maps the transformation of certain medical symptoms – thinness and paleness – into a cultural sign: that of the crisis-woman. Using the tubercular analogy, she shows us how this has already been done for the sanatorium patient – thinness and paleness once signified tubercular – but what makes Nervi distinct is the fact that she is a modern doctor delineating a modern diseased subject, the *donna-crisi*.

Finally, it must be noted that for Lombroso, as for successors such as Pende and Nervi, medical research was closely tied to social control and policing. Lombroso was deeply concerned not only with the prevention of crime but also with the constant management of potential threats to the integrity of the social body. What is especially interesting about his work, however, is the manner in which the body of a woman is subject to discipline in different ways than that of a man. As Horn points out: "The normal woman, a figure that had no real counterpart in Lombroso's studies of male criminality, was ostensibly constructed as a background against which the female offender might become distinct, visible, and legible."[60] But, Horn goes on to argue, "in the end," because his statistics were often numerically insignificant or contradictory, "what emerged from Lombroso's studies was less the (hoped for) transparent pathology of the female offender than the *barely legible potential dangerousness of the normal woman*. As a result ... the *normal woman* was placed at the center of a whole range of modern discourses and technologies ... ranging from social medicine, to social hygiene, to social work."[61] Horn argues that when Lombroso compares the criminal woman, the prostitute, and the normal woman, he views the last as "the most unstable figure because she was physically indistinguishable from the 'occasional criminal'" and was linked to her by the "fund of immorality" latent in all women."[62] "In sum," he concludes, "woman was constructed as both normal in her pathology, and pathological in her normality."[63]

In discussions of the pathological figure of the *donna-crisi* one often sees the very same instability of the boundary between normal and pathological, between self and other, between subject and object that makes not only disciplinary but *self-disciplinary* action so necessary. Nervi's article illustrates this point perfectly. She notes the slippery slope by which a healthy young woman can turn into a crisis-woman: "First, it's the desire not to gain weight so that a dress can fit well, then it's the exaggerated make-up, and then it's following the fashions of society women" [Dapprima è il non volere ingrassare, perché l'abito stia bene, poi il truccarsi esagerato, poi il seguire la moda della donna di società].[64] She goes on to describe the increasing restlessness of young women who can no longer stay at home. They must go to dances, to the theatre, and to other chic locales where they inevitably smoke, drink, and thoroughly exhaust themselves: "They are not few in number, the girls from 15 to 25 years of age that we doctors see 'exhausted,' and it is not due to excessive school programs as their parents lament, but to the excessive fatigue of a fashionable lifestyle" [Non sono poche le ragazze dal 15 ai 25 anni, che noi medici vediamo 'esaurite' e non per gli esagerati programmi scolastici come lamentano i genitori, ma per le esagerate fatiche di una vita di moda].[65] She sums up: "Naturally, then they are pale and they must make themselves up, and they are worn out, and they maintain their flaccid thinness with elastic girdles that damage not only their aesthetic figure but also their internal organs. These are the women who should then transform themselves into good mothers. How can this be possible?" [Naturalmente poi sono pallide e si devono truccare e sono sfinite, e sostengono la loro flaccida magrezza con fasce elastiche che danneggiano, oltre la loro figura estetica, anche i loro organi interni. Queste donne dovrebbero poi tramutarsi in madri e in buone madri. Ma come ciò può essere possibile?].[66]

If we step back to consider for a moment how popular themes appear in scientific writing just as scientific themes appear in popular writing – and, furthermore, how all of these types of writing support the hegemonic ideal of the prolific mother – a larger picture emerges: this phenomenon attests to nothing less than the totalitarian aspirations of the regime. "Fascistization" was a process that concerned *every* domain of life, from enrolment in the PNF and highly visible public displays of loyalty to the regime, to conformity with fascist norms at the most intimate level – correctly choosing everything from the food one ate to the clothes one wore, and undoubtedly privileging the procreative rather than pleasurable aspects of sex. For the lay reader of these popular scientific articles, what is written on the body of the fashionably thin woman is not so much the signs of physical illness (caved-in cheeks or flaccid skin), but the warning that all women – and especially young and naive women – can unsuspectingly cross the line from beauty to ugliness, from health to disease. Most important, however, is the injunction contained in these texts that one must do everything in one's power to protect this from happening.

The Crisis-Woman and Tropes of Disease

As we have seen so far in this chapter, fascist scientific discourse rhetorically attempts to establish a clear link between the crisis-woman and the pathological body: Nervi's article compares the crisis-woman to the pallid tubercular patient while Pende links the "non-maternal female type" to pathological sexual phenomena such as "eunuchs" or "intersexual and virile women." But while fascist scientific discourse seeks to clarify the relation between the thin female body and disease on a medical level (by mapping out definitive symptoms), we might also observe that on a cultural level that discourse paradoxically works to complicate knowledge about this very same body type. Let us begin to tease out the mechanisms and the goals of this operation by looking at yet another of Nicola Pende's articles.

In his brief article entitled "Maternità, estetica e salute femminile" ["Maternity, Aesthetics and Women's Health"] published in December 1934 in *Maternità ed infanzia,* Pende links the thin woman and disease in order to change a perceived social norm. He wants to eradicate the "dangerous prejudice that maternity and childbearing deform the female body, corroding its robustness and longevity" [Il pregiudizio pericoloso che la maternità e la figliolanza deturpino il corpo femminile e ne intacchino la robustezza e la longevità].[67] This destructive and unfounded prejudice, he says, has led married women to "all those practices that impede or strongly limit fecundity" [tutte quelle pratiche che impediscono o limitano fortemente la prolificità] and has led young women to "maintain at all costs the slim and adolescent form of their body" [conservare ad ogni costo la linea snella ed adolescente del loro corpo].[68] Pende severely warns his readers that "nature vindicates itself by creating organic conditions in the voluntarily infertile female organism which, on the one hand, lead to an aesthetic deformation of the body (as they lead to an ethical deformation of the soul) and, on the other hand, lead to certain pathogenic disturbances and illnesses" [la natura si vendica creando nell'organismo femminile volontariamente infecondo condizioni organiche tali, che da un lato portano ad una deformazione estetica del corpo (come portano ad una deformazione etica dell'anima), dall'altro lato determinato disturbi morbosi e malattie].[69] He points to two main "aesthetic deformations": first, sagging skin – especially on the face, breasts, and abdomen – that gives the appearance of premature aging, and second, the growth of facial hair that is typical of women undergoing menopause. Although he leaves to the imagination what the corresponding "ethical deformations of the soul" might be, his list of "pathogenic disturbances and illnesses" – which makes concrete the association between the crisis-woman and disease – is quite detailed: "the voluntary renunciation of maternity creates grave disturbances to the nutrition of the mucous membrane and musculature of the uterus, with hemorrhagic distress or with delay and serious arrest of the menses, and also with the easy development of fibroid tumors" [la rinunzia volontaria alla maternità crea turbamenti gravi della nutrizione della mucosa e della muscolatura dell'utero, con sofferenze emorragiche, o con ritardi ed arresti gravi delle regole, ed anche con facile comparsa di tumori fibromatosi].[70] He continues this list with a series of primarily psychological disturbances:

> it creates psychological and nervous disorders, namely, unrest, cephalic congestion, palpitations, exaggerated reactions to every small annoyance in life, obsessive ideas, periods of depression and dissatisfaction with the self and with those people who surround these poor victims of the mistaken illusion that woman can, without grave physical and moral consequences, betray the divine altruistic mission of perpetuating the species.

> crea disturbi nervosi e psichici, e cioè irrequietezza, cefalee congestizie, palpitazioni, reattività esagerata ad ogni piccola noia della vita, idee ossessive, periodi depressivi di malcontenti di sé e di quelli che circondano queste povere vittime della stola illusione: che la donna possa, senza grave penitenza, fisica e morale, tradire la divina missione altruistica di perpetuare la specie.[71]

In this article, Pende rhetorically attacks what he calls the "dangerous prejudice that maternity and childbearing deform the female body" by arguing that in fact the *opposite* is true: it is the failure to have children that deforms the body, psyche, and soul.

Pende engages here in a gesture of reversal typical of fascist discourse, which Barbara Spackman calls "resemanticization" – a term she uses "to refer to the process by which terms are differently polarized in fascist language: As Mario Isnenghi has noted, what were, in prefascist parlance, positively charged terms now become negatively charged ones."[72] In this case, the once positively charged slim and adolescent-looking non-maternal body is now given a negative charge. It is marked by disease: sagging skin, the premature growth of facial hair, and a variety of "pathenogenic disturbances and illnesses." What is at stake in this resemanticization of the slim body is nothing less than the vernacular redefinition of modern female beauty in healthy, fascist terms rather than traditional, diseased, nineteenth-century terms.

Clark Lawlor's study *Consumption and Literature* provides a historical framework that allows us to better contextualize Pende's resemanticization. He demonstrates the long-standing historical correlation between a linear, thin look and one disease in particular, tuberculosis: "the general shape of the consumptive ... had been a cliché since the classical physicians: long neck, wing-like upper back and thin chest."[73] But even more important is his observation that "by the end of the eighteenth century, consumption is not only the symbolic disease of the lover or a desired condition for the dying Christian, but also the *glamorous sign of female beauty.*"[74] Lawlor provides numerous examples showing that, from the eighteenth century forward, the thin and languid consumptive look was associated with female beauty and upper-class refinement. The fascist science of health and beauty – embodied in the work of Pende and others – attempts to reverse this disease-based model of feminine beauty. It attempts to cast thinness as a sign of physical, racial, moral, and spiritual degeneration and to eliminate any nostalgic longing for the decadent idea of the elite beauty of the bourgeoisie. Fiducia's rhetorical gesture, mentioned above, linking the trend of watching one's waist to the restrictive fashion of the corset – especially popular in the nineteenth century – makes perfect sense when seen in this light.

An equally important framework to consider with regard to Pende's resemanticization is the coding of the severely disciplined thin female body as holy, virtuous, and saintly, as evidenced in European religious writings from the thirteenth century onward. As I mention earlier, within the Catholic paradigm the thin female body historically points to the asceticism and self-restraint of a saint.[75] Indeed, as Carolyn Walker Bynum argues: "Patient suffering of disease or injury was a major way of gaining sanctity for females but not for males."[76] She goes on to say that "not just illness in general but the specific illness of not being able to eat was embraced by medieval women."[77] Pende's resemanticization helps to dismantle this symbolism, especially insofar as he continues to suggest the negative moral implications of thinness.

Irene Brin's characterization of the crisis-woman, however, is particularly interesting because she engages in a slightly different type of resemanticization. Brin draws a distinction between maintaining a healthy, hygienic weight and the potentially fatal error of excessive weight loss. She describes healthy, hygenic weight loss as follows: "Portable scales were produced *en masse* and everyone knew precisely how many hectograms they needed to lose in the course of a day: three spinach-based meals and a twenty-four-hour complete fast were advised for women who had 'gained weight'" [Si producevano in serie le bilance portatili, ognuno sapeva con esattezza quanti etti gli convenisse perdere nel corso della giornata: tre pasti a base di spinaci, un digiuno completo di ventiquattr'ore erano consigliati alle signore che avessero 'acquistato peso'].[78] But she characterizes excessive weight loss quite differently:

> Hollow cheeks, protruding cheekbones, sunken eyes and a bitter smile were not only markers of distinction, but admirable: young girls became

ethereal and got sick to their stomachs. Doctors confirmed that fasting inevitably produced bad breath. Satirical newspapers maligned "Miss Crisis." Everyone knew the tragic end of an ambitious woman; she died, generally, from consumption as a result of having lost too much weight.

> Le gote cave, gli zigomi sporgenti, gli occhi profondi, l'amarezza del sorriso, erano non solo distinti, ma ammirevoli: le fanciulle divenivano eteree e si ammalavano di stomaco. I medici assicuravano che il digiuno procura, inevitabilmente, l'alito fetido: i giornali umoristici deprecavano la "Signorina Crisi." Ognuno conosceva la tragica fine di una donna ambiziosa, morta, generalmente, di consunzione, per esser dimagrita troppo.[79]

Sarcastically poking fun at women who lose too much weight by calling their gruesome physical characteristics "admirable markers of distinction," Brin's resemanticization suggests that consumption is punishment for those who excessively desire glamour rather than a distorted, retrograde sign of glamour as Pende and Fiducia would have it.

While fascist scientific discourse attempted to resemanticize the glamorous nineteenth-century aesthetic of the diseased thin woman and the medieval aesthetic of the saintly thin woman, at the same time it reinforced the link between the excessively thin woman and a host of negative contemporary cultural associations. As the texts I present here show, the crisis-woman can be read as a symbol of many things: bourgeois decadence, egoism, individualism, debauched morals, sexual promiscuity, the perversion of proper sex roles, social upheaval, consumer culture, mass culture, urbanism, anti-naturalism, foreign corruption, physical degeneration, racial degeneration, and the collapse of the nation. This complex and free-flowing interrelated web of negative cultural associations that permeates popular scientific and, to a lesser extent, specialized scientific representations of the crisis-woman shows us how the *donna-crisi* operates through the psychoanalytic mode of condensation with regard to the category of difference. She embodies not just one particular threat but a series of threats – simultaneously. In this sense she operates much like the ideological figure of the Jew in the fascist imagination, who condenses a series of antagonistic qualities (lasciviousness, bodily deformation, financial corruption, moral and religious deviance, and so on) and whose body similarly becomes a symbolic repository for negativity itself.[80]

Furthermore, because condensation is one of the central mechanisms that generates meaning about the crisis-woman in the cultural realm, she is a figure whose negative attributes could be assembled, dismantled, reworked, and rearranged to fit the circumstances. Slender fashion models, women wearing pants instead of skirts, women with boyish haircuts, women engaged in leisure or work activities typical of growing urban centres – these are all women who had the potential to be constituted by and within the figure of the *donna-crisi*. The crisis-woman, in other words, was a figure that served the tactical function of retroactively ascribing ideological value to a host of problematic images of and practices by women. And although any one image may not display all the attributes of the *donna-crisi*, once this epithet marked an image (or person, as the case may be) that image could then signify much more than it depicted. The crisis-woman's variable attributes rendered her an extremely flexible figure that could serve different ideological functions in different contexts: she might have illustrated the necessity of preventing women from working white-collar jobs or from participating in certain sports; she might have reinforced fascist imperialistic desire in the African campaign; she might have underscored the need to stem migration from the countryside to major cities.

It is within the context of this interrelated web of symbols that we can perhaps best understand the popular image of the crisis-woman that has circulated in historical scholarship so far: the 1932 drawing entitled "Cocktail" (Figure 4). On the right, we see an emaciated woman with short hair and a revealing modern dress sitting at a bar and sipping a cocktail from a straw. On the left is a robust and modestly dressed mother nursing a baby in her kitchen. Perhaps, strictly speaking, these antithetical figures should be identified as allegorical representations of the *stracittà* and *strapaese* political movements (which might be translated as the "ultra-urban" and "ultra-local" movements), since they appear in *Il selvaggio*, the mouthpiece of the *strapaesisti* who extolled the pastoral virtues of traditional rural life and sharply criticized the expansion of modern cities. The cocktail – a buzzword and a modern invention tied to consumer culture and decadent femininity – is posited here as the apotheosis of *stracittà*. But the woman representing *strapaese* has redefined the concept by giving her "cocktail" to her child.

One can also see how these two images easily read as representations of the *donna-madre* and the *donna-crisi*. Many of the telltale symptoms and signs of the crisis-woman characterize the figure on the right: excessive thinness and pale cheeks (especially when compared to the woman on the left), egoism (consuming a beverage rather than providing one), perversion of "proper" sex roles (as indicated by the short, mannish hair), sexual promiscuity and debauched morals (as indicated by the revealing dress and consumption of alcohol while sitting alone

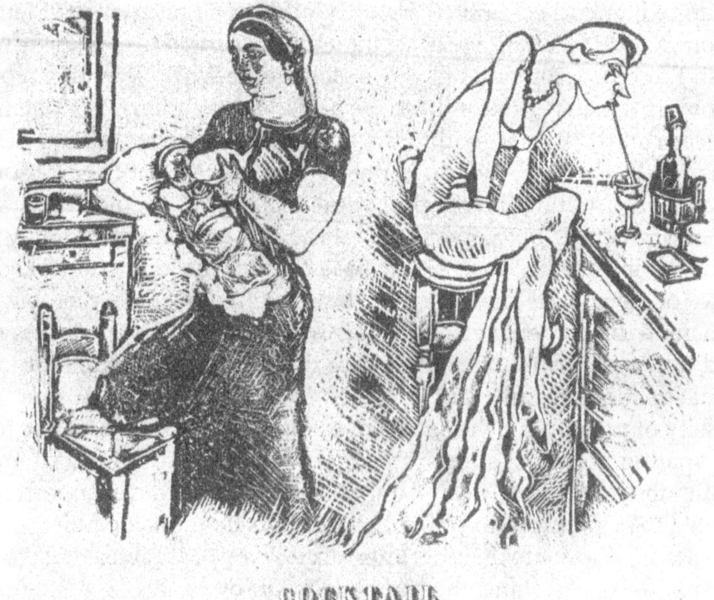

Figure 4. Image from June 1932 issue of *Il Selvaggio*. (By permission of the Ministero dei beni e delle attività culturali e del turismo della Repubblica Italiana / Biblioteca Nazionale Centrale di Firenze. Reproduction prohibited.)

in a public space), urbanism (as indicated by the non-domestic bar setting), and, of course, there is the indicative lack of motherhood (again, when compared to the figure on the left). When we assume that the unnamed figure on the right is a representation of the *donna-crisi* (and that the figure on the left is her counterpart, the *donna-madre*) we illustrate just how the ideological power of the crisis-woman operates. By retroactively naming the figure a crisis-woman, we activate a connotative chain of associations (many of which overlap with those that would be invoked if one were to read the figure strictly as an allegorical representation of *stracittà*) that spell out one major idea – disease – an idea whose power is underwritten by the authority of scientific discourse.

I propose as a concluding thought that the crisis-woman, in all her different pathological inflections – urban, decadent, tubercular, sexually deviant – can be productively read as a concrete embodiment of one overarching trope: the European concept of degeneration that flourished at the end of the nineteenth century. In his excellent comparative study *Faces of Degeneration,* which focuses on the theory of degeneration in the French, Italian, and British contexts, Daniel Pick explains: "The term *dégénérescence*" was "developed in a later-nineteenth-century European psychiatry 'obsessed' with the naming and fixing of conditions."[81] "*Dégénérescence,*" he continues, "was more than just another mental condition to set alongside the others in an interminable *psychopathia sexualis*; it became indeed the condition of conditions, the ultimate signifier of pathology."[82] Although degeneration came out of the psychiatric context, "it was a shifting term produced, inflected, refined, and re-constituted in the movement between the human sciences, fictional narratives and socio-political commentaries."[83] Likewise, Robert Nye observes that in France, "by the 1890s, the theory [of degeneration] was being widely employed as an explanation for the whole range of pathologies from which the nation suffered: alcoholism, prostitution and pornography, suicide, and the incapacity (or unwillingness) to procreate."[84] The crisis-woman, we might say, was degeneration reincarnate in the twentieth century and summed up into a tangible and – presumably with the help of fascist policy – eradicable type. But the gravity of the crisis-woman's condition was not immutable, as we shall see in the next chapter on satirical cartoons – indeed a little levity was a necessary release for the social integration of such a wretched figure.

3

Esci fuori, mattacchiona!: Satirical Representations of the Donna-crisi

In 1933, as the campaign against the crisis-woman reached its peak, citizens walking along the streets of Italy's capital city might well have heard someone whistling Romolo Balzani's catchy new tune "Donna crisi."[1] This song, sung by the popular singer in his native earthy Roman dialect, shows him trying to convince his sweetheart to abandon her "Hollywood" dieting regime: "You seemed so beautiful to me/when you were a bit chubby!/But when we go out, with the waist that you've got now/I feel like I'm carrying around a bamboo cane!" [A me parevi invece tanto bella/ quann'eri un pochettino grassottella!/E quanno uscimo insieme co' la vita che ciài tu/ me pare che me porto er bastoncino de bambù!].[2] In an attempt to change her mind, Balzani unfavourably compares his lover to a bamboo cane, a candlewick, and a bone, and makes it clear that he would rather have a "steak filet" [bistecca ar filoncino] – in short, something into which he can really sink his teeth. He concludes the song with a catchy and memorable rhyme that, due to its impersonal grammatical construction, seems very much like a dictum aimed not only at his lover but to all of his listeners: "The crisis-woman isn't pretty/One needs a woman made like a sandwich!" [la donna crisi nun è bella/ce vò 'na donna fatta a pagnottella!].[3] Balzani's song typifies the manner in which the *donna-crisi* was portrayed by satirical fascist propaganda: she was a useless, undesirable, and passive figure that was always the butt of a joke.

Only two years before Balzani's song hit the charts, Press Office minister Gaetano Polverelli issued his directive to stop printing images of the dangerously thin crisis-woman and start printing sketches that disparaged her. Notably, among the first publications to respond to Polverelli's call were Italy's satirical gazettes. Almost at once, the pages of *Il Travaso, Marc'Aurelio,* and many other *giornali satirici e umoristici* began to fill with propagandistic satirical cartoons that, like Balzani's song, ridiculed the newly emerged, so-called anti-demographic crisis-woman. They poked fun at her stick-like figure, mocked her lack of sex appeal, cast her as a domineering wife and inadequate mother, and generally portrayed her as a thoroughly unlikable character. The quickness of their response was no doubt linked to the fact that the ridicule of women was nothing new for this type of publication. For many decades, women – especially those who dared to question or disregard social mores – had been the frequent object of their mockery.[4] The emancipated "modern woman," whom I describe in chapter 1, and the militant suffragette were two of their many targets. Satirical gazettes found ample fodder for their lampoons of the *donna-crisi* in part by recycling hackneyed tropes about women that had circulated throughout the previous century and in part by inventing new ones. Polverelli must have been pleased by this efficiency, not least because the satirical cartoon had long been recognized by bureaucrats just like him as a useful tool to shape public opinion.

This chapter examines representations of the *donna-crisi* in the cartoons of Italian satirical gazettes published in the early 1930s. It is divided into three main sections, the first of which provides a general overview of the texts examined and frames them as a type of subtle but persuasive propaganda. The second section delves into a close reading of individual cartoons, describes the linguistic mechanisms through which humour about the crisis-woman functions in these texts, and explains the ideological function of this humour. Although the linguistic blunders and funny gaffes proposed by these verbal and visual texts may seem light-hearted and inconsequential, I argue that they in fact perform the ideological work of "interpellating the hegemonic subject" who laughs in agreement with fascist ideals.[5] What is especially interesting about these cartoons is the manner in which they might be read against the grain of their propagandistic intent. The final section, therefore, focuses on subversive rather than hegemonizing humour, and teases out the possibilities as well as the limitations of a type of laughter that escapes fascist control.

Satirical Cartoons as Propaganda

Disparaging cartoons of the *donna-crisi,* found in Italian satirical gazettes, typify the manner in which fascist propaganda could be extremely subtle rather than heavy-handed, especially during the first decade of the *ventennio*. They are excellent illustrations of what French philosopher Jacques Ellul calls the "propaganda of integration," which "aims at making the individual participate in his society in every way" and "seeks to obtain stable behaviour, to adapt the individual to his everyday life, to reshape his thoughts and behaviour in terms of the permanent social setting."[6] "Integration propaganda," Ellul writes, "aims at stabilizing the social body, at unifying it and reinforcing it."[7] Historian Philip Cannistraro sheds further light on Ellul's notion when he writes: "This new type of propaganda – acting indirectly through the dominant climate and atmosphere in the country, and seeking to influence people through their customs, habits, and unconscious behavior – harmonizes very well with Mussolini's goals. The end result of a propaganda such as this is to create progressive adaptation to a given way of life" – which would, of course, be a *fascist* way of life.[8] Cannistraro concludes that "there is no doubt that in 1927 this type of propaganda had already become, within the fascist regime, deliberate and systematic."[9] According to him, the regime concerned itself with two major types of "propaganda of integration" during its first decade: propaganda relating to the image of Mussolini, and that relating to the image of a New Italy. He views the campaign against the *donna-crisi* – or, in his words, the campaign against "excessively and artificially thin women, or those with a masculine appearance, or additionally, those that represent a 'sterile' type of woman" – as part of the drive to create a New Italy with new social mores.[10] It is within this framework that I consider the artistic production of satirical gazettes.

Together with women's magazines, satirical gazettes are the chief sources for primary material on the *donna-crisi*. This is a significant and perhaps surprising discovery, since well-known scholars like Elisabetta Mondello argue that negative representations of the *donna-crisi* are most commonly found in a very different type of publication. "We should not be surprised," writes Mondello, "that the battle against models of femininity deemed unacceptable and dangerous by the regime … was entrusted to important official publications like *Critica fascista* or *La stirpe*. To be sure, at first sight, headlines against the *donna-crisi* (this was the expression then in use), considered to be the negation of the *donna-madre*, appear incongruous here."[11] My research, however, shows that – when compared to popular publications like fashion magazines and satirical gazettes – references to the crisis-woman are notably absent from "official publications," which instead focus almost exclusively on the "positive" model of the prolific mother. Mondello is not alone in overlooking satirical gazettes as a rich source of primary material on the *donna-crisi*. The cartoons I present here have not been discussed by any other scholar working on representations of femininity during the fascist period, despite the fact that they appeared in widely read publications.[12]

Because satirical cartoons originate in the popular press rather than in more specialized publications, they are texts that shed important light on the manner in which the crisis-woman functioned as an instrument of propaganda. Rather than heavy-handed and fear-inducing condemnations, one finds, in these drawings, only clumsy jokes and tempered ridicule. But the light-hearted laughter provoked by these jokes was a vital mechanism used to convince the general public of the common-sense validity of fascist ideals. In short, these cartoons, as examples of a propaganda of integration, present a type of hegemonizing humour that was important to the advancement of fascist notions of femininity and, more generally, of the social norms that the regime supported. Laughter can be an undeniably powerful social, cultural, and even political force. As Mary Douglas points out in her study of the joke as rite: "public joking, shared laughter, and celebration of agreement on what deserves ridicule and affirmation fosters community and furthers a sense of mutual support for common belief and behavior."[13] Or, to put it a bit differently using the terminology of political scientist Joseph Nye, one can say that an analysis of these cartoons reveals the importance of the persuasive operations of "soft" rather than "hard" power in disseminating and reinforcing fascist ideals.[14] If all of Italy was laughing at the crisis-woman, then one surely wants to know just what was so funny.

The Politics of Satire: Not Necessarily Subversive

The cartoons in this chapter are all free-standing drawings with a caption, and are examples of what I shall call propagandistic social satire. They were typical of satirical gazettes in Italy and Europe from the nineteenth century forward, and they primarily commented on social mores and political events.[15] Following the work of Linda Hutcheon, we can define satire as a genre, and more specifically as a subgenre of the comic.[16] Hutcheon argues that satire's "ethos" is best characterized as "scornful" or "disdainful."[17] But lest we misunderstand satire's disdain, she stresses that "the *corrective aim* of satire's scornful ridicule is central to its identity. While satire can be destructive, there is also an *implied idealism*, for it is often 'unabashedly didactic and seriously committed to a hope in its own power to effect change.'"[18] The intent of satire, then, is ameliorative – even if at first sight it seems primarily disparaging. Within this framework, the cartoons in this chapter are examples of *propagandistic* social satire because they conform to the regime's dictates. Their "corrective aim" is directed at the trend of thinning down, which fascism viewed as a threat to the nation-as-body. If it is true, as Hutcheon argues, that satire can be used not only to subvert but to "defend norms," and that it often "ridicules in order to bring deviation into line," then one can see how the genre perfectly lends itself to the realization of Polverelli's dictates.[19]

This view of satire clashes with that of scholars who believe that the genre inherently questions hegemonic structures of power. For example, one of the best-known Italian historians of the *giornali satirici e umoristici*, Enrico Gianeri, writes in his impressive tome *Storia della caricatura europea* that "satire or caricature, which is *fundamentally and by nature democratic if it is authentic*, has widely contributed to the Resistance with clandestine caricaturists who heeded no danger, polemical designers of underground pamphlets, and courageous combatants."[20] Indeed, in the section of his book that focuses on the fascist period, Gianeri – himself a left-wing illustrator who published in these years under the pen name "GEC" – gives his reader the impression that satire was a domain of political critique exclusively wielded by antifascists and other political resistors. He even goes so far as to suggest that fascism as a cultural phenomenon was inherently opposed to satire: "Like the clericalism that preceded it ... fascism too was absolutely incapable of producing satire worthy of consideration. It was allergic to humor."[21]

Historian Claudio Carabba paints a picture that is more satisfyingly complex. He says: "one will always find people on different sides of the fence: Galantra with Calarini [two left-wing satirists] who defend the values of the great progressive and socialist utopias against the fascists with a black shirt and a billy club of *420* [a fascist satirical gazette]."[22] Carabba makes a distinction that is more useful than Gianeri's contrast between "authentic" satire and that not "worthy of consideration": "Humorists, ... perhaps with faulty approximation, can be divided into two general categories: the 'rebels,' the resistors to the heavy hand of power, and the obliging 'jokers' who, with an air of mocking and poking fun, do nothing but preserve intact the prejudices of a rigidly constituted order."[23]

Here we shall examine the artistic production of the "jokers" rather than the "rebels," and focus on three popular gazettes, *Il Travaso, Marc'Aurelio,* and *Settebello.* Of the three, *Il Travaso* has the longest and most illustrious history.[24] It first came out around 1900 and stopped publishing over half a century later in 1962. Its list of distinguished collaborators includes some of the greatest artists in the field: Livio Apolloni, Guglielmo Guasta, Filiberto Scarpelli, Toddi (Pietro Silvio Rivetta di Solonghello), and Yambo (Enrico Novelli), among many others. *Marc'Aurelio* was published out of Rome and was named after the classical equestrian statue that crowns the Capitoline Hill.[25] It was founded in 1931 and was immediately recognized for its innovative designs and humour. In its long list of notable collaborators one finds, among others, the name of Federico Fellini, who worked for the publication before he turned to film-making. The third gazette, *Settebello,* was established in 1933 and in the latter part of the decade was famously co-directed by the writer-screenwriter duo Achille Campanile and Cesare Zavattini. I will also consider several cartoons by the artist Paolo Garretto that, according to Gianeri, originally appeared in a lesser-known gazette called *Fuorisacco* and were collected and published together in a free-standing pamphlet entitled *Donne-crisi.*[26] Although each of these gazettes has its distinct characteristics, writers and illustrators frequently moved back and forth between them and worked collaboratively. This group of texts can therefore be taken as representative of a larger artistic milieu that includes the cinematic, theatrical, and literary spheres – as the names above suggest. And, as the lyrics of the Balzani song that open this chapter show, these texts also influenced the world of popular music that stemmed from the tradition of the *café-chantant.* Finally, it is worth pointing out that, although I have limited my sources out of necessity, one finds lampoons of the crisis-woman in nearly every satirical gazette published in Italy between 1931 and 1933.

Although the satirical gazettes in this chapter clearly reinforce the regime's strategic disparagement of the *donna-crisi,* they should be distinguished from philofascist satirical gazettes – such as *420* and *Matamoro* – that in every issue unabashedly extolled the virtues of Mussolini and the blackshirts. But *Il Travaso, Marc'Aurelio,* and *Settebello* are also not like Italy's antifascist "rebel" gazettes that dared to openly and savagely critique the regime. These were either closed down or forced into exile during the brutal 1925 crackdown on the press.[27] One example of such a "rebel" gazette is the celebrated and searingly critical *Il becco giallo,* whose symbolic mascot under fascist rule was a blackbird with a locked beak. It was predictably censored, moved to France, and sent clandestine copies into fascist Italy until 1931, when it ceased publication altogether.[28] If the satirical gazettes examined here cannot properly be categorized as philofascist or antifascist, neither can they be classified as neutral. Instead, they represent a type of cultural production that operated within an ambiguous "grey zone," to use Primo Levi's term.[29] Many emerged after the dictatorship, and all learned how to survive within a system of censorship that could be as brutal as it was unpredictable.[30] I agree with Levi that morally complex situations call for morally complex responses. In this case, one must theorize gradations of political support rather than look for an unambiguous fascist or antifascist position. Moreover, one must keep in mind that political discourse of *any* kind is rarely logical, straightforward, or free of contradiction. The readings offered in this chapter therefore attend to the ways in which language and image in these cartoons both support and occasionally subvert fascist values; they focus on the political narratives these texts offer as well as those they undermine.

The Articulation of Wit

Today, satirical gazettes of the fascist period can be found in many places: in the echoing, solemn halls of Italy's national libraries; in the extensive collections of its Museum of Satire and Caricature; in the country's numerous, overcrowded, musty antiquarian bookshops; and in the open-air book stalls of bustling flea markets in cities large and small. Any person inclined to leaf through the pages of these diverting publications will notice recurrent cartoons that mock the *donna-crisi* in the issues of the early 1930s. A closer look will show that the witticisms offered by such cartoons overwhelmingly function through one main rhetorical device: the double entendre. Some cartoons use words like "bastoncino" [slender stick] or "chiodo" [nail] to humorously and simultaneously evoke an object and the thin body of the crisis-woman. In one cartoon, the skinny *donna-crisi* is cleverly said to "fare una magra figura" ["to cut a poor figure" or, literally, "to make a thin figure"]. In another, a male singer who has wed a crisis-woman is said to have made the error of "prendere una stecca" ["hitting a bad note" or, literally, "picking out a stick"].[31] Given the oral culture associated with jokes – which are designed to pass from person to person as they are told and retold – one can argue that the wordplay in these satirical cartoons, in effect, functions as a mnemonic device that links various epithets with the figure of the crisis-woman. When speaking of this female type, one could – and many texts from this period *did* – refer not only to a "donna-crisi" but to "un'alice" [an anchovy], "un'assicella" [a thin plank], "un'ossa" [a bone], and so on. As this chapter unfolds, we shall see how the double entendre and its relative the pun are mechanisms central to the propagandistic intent of these satirical cartoons.

Interestingly enough, many of these cartoons are characterized by a tautological rather than incongruous relationship between image and text. Since most turn on *verbal* rather than visual jokes, rarely does the caption of a cartoon fundamentally alter one's understanding of the image. Instead, the graphic design simply underscores or repeats a clever play on words.[32] Indeed, without the linguistic witticism, most of these cartoons would lose their "punch," so to speak. Take, for example, Umberto Onorato's drawing entitled "Amuleti" [Lucky Charms], which decorates the cover of *Il Travaso* in December 1932 (Figure 5). This cartoon shows a well-dressed man in a chic, modern, bourgeois salon. He chats with three equally well-dressed women over a cup of tea, and has a concerned or perhaps embarrassed expression on his face. The women, instead, smile at him, bend towards him, and gesture in an animated fashion. In the background, one notices that a stylish, thin, and frowning woman – the *donna-crisi* – has just entered the house and is being received by a butler. This entire scene is framed on the left by a tied-back curtain. Suspended above, and out of the picture, are a series of good luck charms hanging on a string. This image is quite undecipherable as a joke about the crisis-woman without the caption below it, the man's confession to the group: "I married a woman as thin as a nail, but she didn't bring me luck" [Ho sposato una donna magra come un chiodo, ma non mi ha portato fortuna.] The joke here is not visual but verbal, and turns on the double meaning of the word "nail": a nail is a lucky charm in Italy, but it also refers here to the thin silhouette of the *donna-crisi*. This poor husband's "good luck charm" has brought him nothing but misfortune, as his wife's unpleasant frown suggests.

It is Freud who reminds us that humour lies in the *articulation* of a joke rather than in its content. When speaking of the "linguistic or expressive technique" of a joke, he says it "must be intimately related to [the joke's] essential nature, for jokiness and its effect vanish when [the joke's] wording is replaced by something different."[33] He argues that, like the process of dreamwork, the joke relies on linguistic mechanisms to create meaning. In the case of "Amuleti" the mechanism is the

Figure 5. "Amuleti" [Lucky Charms] by Umberto Onorato for *Il Travaso* (18 December 1932). The caption reads: "I married a woman as thin as a nail but she didn't bring me luck!" (By permission of the Ministero dei beni e delle attività culturali e del turismo della Repubblica Italiana/Biblioteca Nazionale Centrale di Firenze. Reproduction prohibited.)

double meaning of the word "nail." But although the central mechanism of the joke in this cartoon is verbal rather than visual, it does not function through wordplay alone. The image, or the mise en scène, of this joke is also crucial to its meaning. If one joins the caption with the picture, then one arrives at a fuller understanding of this man's rather vague bad luck: the arrival of his crisis-wife on the scene negates the fortune of the man's current situation, namely, to be surrounded by three attractive and smiling women who, judging by their body language, seem extremely well-disposed to him.[34] This scenario evokes the familiar trope of the wife as symbol for the loss of man's freedom. As Umberto Eco puts it in *A Theory of Semiotics*: "The woman, the moment she becomes 'wife,' is no longer merely a physical body: she is a *sign* which connotes a system of social obligations."[35] At the same time, the cartoon implicitly suggests the inability of the crisis-wife to sexually satisfy her husband, who turns hopefully towards other women – a recurrent theme in these cartoons, as I discuss below.

In thinking about the articulation of this joke, however, we must draw attention to the fact that its humour turns on an exaggeration of the literal rather than figurative meaning of the word "nail." What is funny here is that a woman could literally be so thin as to be exchanged for a nail. The added irony – to which everyone but the crisis-woman herself is privy – is that this excessively thin woman only differs from a nail insofar as she fails to bring luck. This mode of articulation, which hyperbolizes the literal function of language, is also present in cartoons that pun on idiomatic expressions, such as those mentioned in passing above. In "Crocodile Tears" [Lagrime di coccodrilla] by Vera D'Angara, the *donna-crisi* uses literal rather than figurative language when she speaks of her "figura magra" (Figure 6). The fuller-figured women, in contrast, are capable of *reversing* the word order of the crisis-woman's speech to form an idiomatic expression ("fare una magra figura") that cleverly refers back to her. While this second group of women skillfully employ figurative language, the crisis-woman is distinguished by the manner in which she fails to do so and can only embody the literal meaning of a word or expression. She is a laughable figure because she is completely unaware that she *cuts* a "magra figura" at the same time that she *is* a "figura magra." Similarly, while the tenor in Cesare Gobbo's "Crisis-Woman" cartoon may have figuratively "hit a wrong note" [preso una stecca] by marrying an extremely thin woman, the humour of the cartoon lies in the fact that his skinny crisis-wife embodies the *literal* qualities of his mistake insofar as she is as thin as a stick or "stecca" (Figure 7).

Figure 6. "Lagrime di coccodrilla" [Crocodile Tears] by Vera d'Angara for *Il Travaso* (26 March 1933). The caption reads: "I've made so many sacrifices in order to have a thin figure! …" "And now you do nothing but cut a bad figure!" (By permission of the Ministero dei beni e delle attività culturali e del turismo della Repubblica Italiana/Biblioteca Nazionale Centrale di Firenze. Reproduction prohibited.)

This repeated emphasis on literalism most often works to discursively position the crisis-woman as object rather than subject. Here I give only two examples – that of a nail and a stick – but cartoonists have

La donna crisi

IL MAESTRO BARILLI: — Da quando vi siete sposato vi vedo triste. Che vi accade?

IL TENORE: — Non vedete! Ho preso una stecca!

Figure 7. "La donna crisi" [The Crisis-Woman] by Cesare Gobbo for *Settebello* (21 May 1933). The caption reads: Maestro Barilli: "I notice that you've been sad since you've gotten married. What is the problem?" The tenor: "Don't you see? I've hit a false note!" (By permission of the Ministero dei beni e delle attività culturali e del turismo della Repubblica Italiana/Biblioteca Nazionale Centrale di Firenze. Reproduction prohibited.)

chosen many other objects, including a toothpick, a pole, a thin plank, a coat rack, a bus stop, and the list goes on. It would seem that any long and slender object is fair game for their jokes. As an object rather than a subject, the crisis-woman rarely speaks and is more often spoken about.

When she does speak, as in D'Angara's "Crocodile Tears," she frequently misuses language or – as the title suggests – her words are as false as her tears. In sum, she is a laughable figure because she does not shape but is *shaped by* a series of visual and verbal signs that are beyond her comprehension and control. The reader, on the other hand, is privy to the workings of language and to the multiple layers of meaning that make the humoristic exchange or misreading of signs possible. Access to this knowledge puts the reader in a position to laugh at the *donna-crisi*, often in chorus with others in the imagined scene.

But the one "misreading" that the laughing reader blindly participates in, and that always remains unquestioned in these cartoons, is the exchange of woman for object. Without fail, these cartoons take for granted the validity of exchanging the thin crisis-woman for a similarly shaped object and consistently disavow the fact that the exchange of a woman for an object must necessarily occur at the figurative level: if these cartoons are to retain their humour, then the crisis-woman can only *embody the qualities* of various long and slender objects, but can never *actually be* those objects.

Disavowal, Displacement, and the Humour of Dis-identification

In order to further explore the various mechanisms of disavowal that operate in these cartoons, let us look at another image that depicts the crisis-woman as object: Paolo Garretto's untitled 1933 drawing in which a myopic man mistakes a crisis-woman for an umbrella (Figure 8). Although there is no linguistic play on words here, the image presents a visual double entendre. The angry crisis-woman is almost exactly the same triangular shape as the two umbrellas in the cartoon: her geometrical clothing makes her shoulders square and broad while, in contrast, her legs are slim and her toes pointed; the vertical folds at the bottom of her dress recall those of the man's umbrella in the rack next to her; the ruffles at her neckline recall those of the woman's umbrella that she firmly clutches in her right hand; finally, to complete the picture, her turned head looks uncannily like the handle of an umbrella. The reader is called upon to laugh here not so much at the social gaffe, or at the awkward man who commits it, as at the outrageous contour of the crisis-woman's silhouette. Indeed, the mistaken exchange of woman for object is cast as quite understandable, given the undeniable similarities between the shape of the crisis-woman and the shape of the umbrella, which even a myopic reader can plainly see. What is most

Il signore miope. — *Scusi tanto, signorina, credevo foss l'ombrello!*

Figure 8. Untitled. Paolo Garretto (1933). The caption reads: The near-sighted man: "Many apologies, Miss, I thought you were my umbrella!" (By permission of the Ministero dei beni e delle attività culturali e del turismo della Repubblica Italiana/Biblioteca Nazionale Centrale di Firenze. Reproduction prohibited.)

ridiculous is the woman herself, whose face clearly shows her misguided anger at being taken for an umbrella.

One of the elements that distinguishes this cartoon from others like it is that the *donna-crisi* is exchanged for a culturally coded object that is markedly less banal than a nail, a stick, a toothpick, or a coat rack. Throughout the eighteenth and nineteenth centuries, the umbrella was an exclusive commodity that symbolized the wealth and aristocracy of the urban upper classes. By the start of the twentieth century, however, it was produced for less money on a larger scale. No longer specially made for a select group, the umbrella was readily available to the middle and lower classes and, in general, was seeing the end of its era as a stylish accessory.[36] A reading of this object within its historical context reveals that underlying the humorous exchange of the crisis-woman for an umbrella is a distinct anxiety about the potential blurring of class lines and the levelling of subject positions that accompanied the rise of consumer culture. Moreover, when carefully considered, the umbrella in this cartoon reveals not only shifting signifiers of class but also shifting signifiers of gender. The umbrella was coded as more masculine than the increasingly rare parasol. The fact that the crisis-woman in Garretto's cartoon is drawn to be more like the *man's* umbrella for which she is mistaken than her own petite and parasol-like feminine umbrella suggests her infamous and distasteful "masculinity," which was commonly decried in fascist dictates.[37]

In Garretto's cartoon, then, the mechanism of disavowal functions on three levels. First, there is the disavowal of the subjectivity of the crisis-woman, since the unquestioned exchange of woman for object grounds the humour of this sketch. This disavowal, in turn, displaces two more: the disavowal of the possibility that one class can be taken for another, and the disavowal of the possibility that a woman can be taken for a man. The threatening blurring of class lines and markers of gender is tamed and displaced by the non-threatening blurring of woman and object. Moreover, the substitution of woman for object – in particular, that of woman for *commodity* – should be understood as a singularly non-threatening exchange in part because it is so familiar. Indeed, feminist scholars have pointed out that contemporary society as a whole is founded upon this transaction.[38] For example, Luce Irigaray states in her chapter of *This Sex Which Is Not One* entitled "Women on the Market" that "women's bodies – through their use, consumption, and circulation – provide for the condition making social life and culture possible."[39] Pointing to the writings of Levi-Strauss and Marx, Irigaray shows how the exchange of women-as-commodity is one of the most basic elements of patriarchal society, so much so that it has become completely naturalized and unremarkable. It is precisely this exchange that enables the hegemonizing humour of Garretto's cartoon.

Even though this cartoon and others like it describe a process of misrecognition, misidentification, and shifting of meaning, there is never any doubt here about the key figure of dis-identification. In Garretto's illustration and others, it is always the crisis-woman who remains firmly outside the bounds of cultural intelligibility. She is always the unassuming target of humour rather than the knowing subject who laughs, and it is in this sense that each of these satirical cartoons validate fascist ideals: their "corrective aim" is directed against the modern trend of thinning down, and the light-hearted laughter they provoke reinforces the supposed common-sense belief that women need to be round-bodied to be beautiful, to be healthy, and to satisfy male desire. Women, such as the crisis-woman, who fail to meet this criterion are depicted as completely and utterly abject; they are undesirable in every imaginable way. Indeed, they are inhuman objects rather than sentient subjects. To acknowledge a crisis-woman as a subject would be to problematically point to a misreading on the part of the reader and would in fact *redirect* laughter; its object would no longer be the crisis-woman but someone else, such as the person who has bought the gazette for a laugh, presumably at another's expense. Thus, the disavowal of the crisis-woman as subject must stay firmly in place since it forms the foundation of the subject who laughs at the joke that is in line with fascist humour, and it underlies the fantasy of shared laughter, or "celebration of agreement," that is at the heart of the convincing "propaganda of integration" of this particular set of cultural texts.

To further illustrate this last point, let us look at an unusual cartoon by Mameli Barbara, entitled "Donna crisi utilitaria" ["The Utilitarian Crisis-Woman"], which appeared in *Marc'Aurelio* in April 1933 (Figure 9; captions in Appendix C). This cartoon stands out from the group because it tells a story by using a series of sequenced images, each with long captions written in rhyming tetrameter. As Barbara's title suggests, his drawing is an illustration of how a crisis-woman might be useful. The story focuses on the trials and tribulations of a certain resourceful Mr Pasquale. In the first two frames we see Mr Pasquale turning the date on his calendar to April 21 – fascist labour day – and immediately being confronted with a problem: he cannot fly his flag on this important national holiday because he has no staff from which to

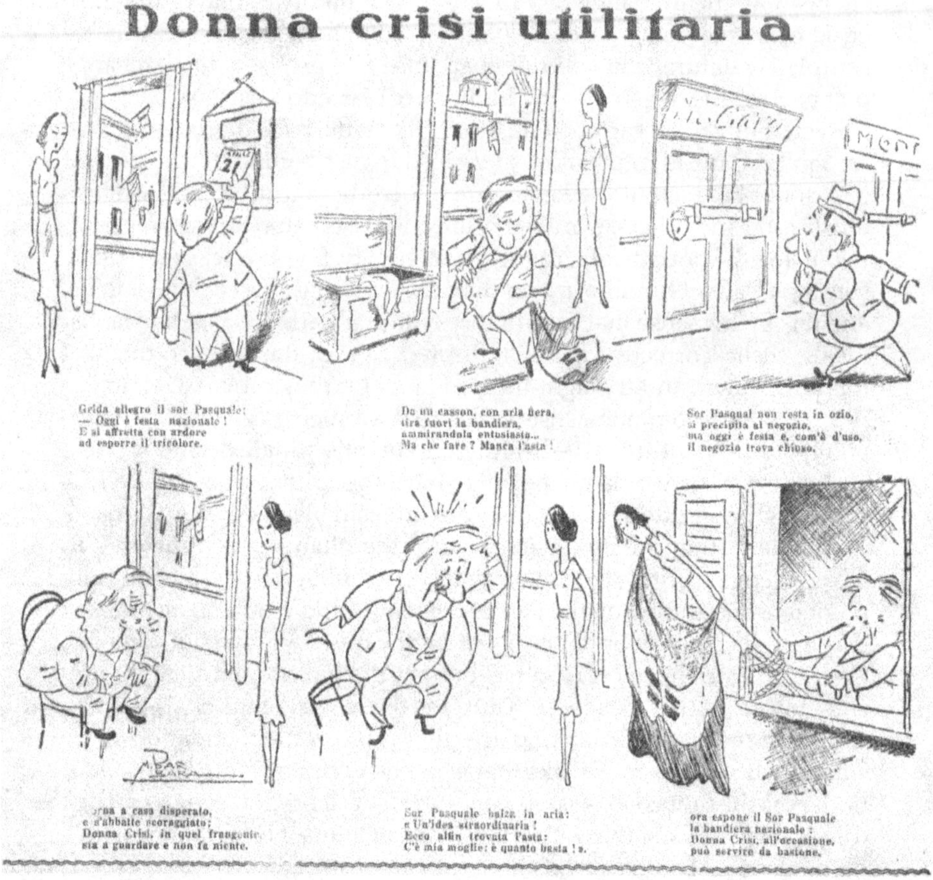

Figure 9. "Donna crisi utilitaria" [Utilitarian Crisis Woman]. Mameli Barbara for *Marc'Aurelio* (5 April 1933). See Appendix C for captions. (By permission of the Ministero dei beni e delle attività culturali e del turismo della Repubblica Italiana/Biblioteca Nazionale Centrale di Firenze. Reproduction prohibited.)

hang it.[40] The epithets used to characterize the crisis-woman described so far make it easy to guess what rhyming solution he finds: "Here at last is found a staff:/There's my wife: and she's enough!" [Ecco alfin trovata l'asta:/C'è mia moglie: è quanto basta!]. The last image in the series shows his wife, the crisis-woman, hanging out of the window

– straight-bodied and looking just a bit surprised – with the waving flag attached to her neck at one end and to her hand at the other: "Now Mr. Pasquale displays/the flag of our nation:/Crisis Woman can serve as a staff/for this occasion" [Ora espone il Sor Pasquale/ la bandiera nazionale:/ Donna Crisi, all'occasione,/ può servire da bastone].

In an interesting departure from the objects described until now, the body of the *donna-crisi* here becomes a mount here for a *national* and *fascist* emblem. This seems to have been a popular motif; it also appears, for example, in Romolo Balzani's song "Donna Crisi" – quoted at the start of this chapter – which goes: "To be honest, what can I do with you? I'll use you as a staff for a flag!" [Co' te che posso facce a esse sincera? T'adoperò pe' asta de bandiera!] (see Appendix B for lyrics). Rather than the usual mistaken exchange of crisis-woman for object, in this cartoon we see an innovative and unusual substitution of the crisis-woman for a missing and needed object. This substitution is all the more ingenious since the crisis-woman – who stands for everything that is non-fascist – for once serves her nation and state. Although she can't make babies like the *donna-madre*, and she can't be an icon of fascist style like the athletic fascist "new woman" – indeed, she can't even help her husband think of a solution to his dilemma – at least she can be a flagpole on this special day. Only in this way can she become a culturally valuable and productive body in fascist terms, although not so much a body that symbolizes national identity as one that sustains it.

Interestingly, the crisis-woman is not the only source of laughter here. There is something undeniably comic about Mr Pasquale. In addition to his slightly disheveled and ridiculous appearance, he is completely oblivious to the fact that the solution he has devised is as absurd as it is ingenious. But, just as Garretto's umbrella cartoon encourages the reader to laugh at the crisis-woman rather than at the myopic man, the reader here is positioned to laugh at the errors of the crisis-woman over the obliviousness of Mr Pasquale. The crisis-woman, as usual, evokes laughter because despite the fact that she is as thin as a flag-pole she cannot imagine that she could be used as one. On the other hand, although Mr Pasquale laughably fails to see his idea as far-fetched, he is distinguished from the crisis-woman insofar as he *actually develops* a solution to his problem; he *actually invents* utility where there was none. And – this is the catch – it *actually works*! The reader is asked to suspend all disbelief as the crisis-woman is hung out the window in the final frame. Moreover, from a fascist perspective, Mr Pasquale's absurdity is entirely comprehensible since it is carried out in the name of the state.

It is his patriotism, which knows no bounds, that leads him to his inventive solution; his nationalistic ardour might just as well be summed up in Mussolini's now infamous refrain: "Everything in the state, nothing outside the state, nothing against the state" [Tutto nello stato, niente al di fuori dello stato, nulla contro lo stato].

Aside from its unusual formal structure and its distinctive trope of the ingenious idea (rather than the understandable gaffe or the amusing coincidence), what distinguishes this cartoon from others like it is the fact that Mr Pasquale's idea pushes the exchange of crisis-woman for object to an extreme. Although the husband in "Amuleti" points to the similarities and ironic differences between his wife and a nail, he never attempts to use his wife as a nail. And although the myopic man in Garretto's cartoon mistakes the crisis-woman for an umbrella, he does not go on to use her as one. But in Barbara's cartoon, the unthinkable happens. The intentionality of this final "utilitarian" act exposes the fantasy of violence against the crisis-woman that runs throughout these satirical cartoons. This fantasy is deferred in Garretto's illustration: we see the moment *after* the myopic man has touched the crisis-woman in an unwelcome fashion with his extended, over-sized, groping hand. In Barbara's cartoon, however, the fantasy is played out: the flag has almost become the noose of the *donna-crisi* and her body is bound by the cords that her husband pulls tight in the last frame.

Satirical Cartoons as Propaganda of Integration

Many of the cartoons in Italy's satirical gazettes do not have such overtly patriotic themes as "La donna crisi utilitaria." Indeed, most are more subtle in their political propositions, and yet they still work to interpellate a subject who laughs in agreement with fascist ideals. Let us turn now to a cartoon that functions a bit differently than those I have described so far: Vera d'Angara's illustration entitled "La donna-crisi" published in September 1932 in *Il Travaso* (Figure 10). D'Angara was one of the few successful female cartoonists in this period, and this example of her work uses the common play on the word "crisis." Although there is no exchange of crisis-woman for object here, she is identified with something more abstract: the economic crisis. The cartoon shows a thin and a full-figured woman waiting for a boat in front of a poster advertising the "Eastern Fair" [La fiera del levante]. This large commercial fair, held in the city of Bari on Italy's eastern coast, was designed to promote trade and financial development in southern Italy, and is still today a major annual event. It was championed by fascism as an

Figure 10. "La donna-crisi" by Vera d'Angara for *Il Travaso* (11 September 1932). The caption reads: "You want to go to the Fiera del Levante? Don't hope for success! Who do you think is going to notice a "crisis" down there?" (By permission of the Ministero dei beni e delle attività culturali e del turismo della Repubblica Italiana/Biblioteca Nazionale Centrale di Firenze. Reproduction prohibited.)

example of the regime's economic success in a period of worldwide financial decline. In d'Angara's cartoon, the full-figured woman says to the thin one: "You want to go to the Fiera del Levante? Don't hope for success! Who do you think is going to notice a 'crisis' down there?" [Vuoi andare alla Fiera del Levante? Non sperare di aver successo! Chi vuoi che laggiù si accorga della "crisi"?]. The play on words here is easy to understand: "crisis" figuratively alludes to the economic crisis of the early 1930s and to the woman herself. Both will fail to be noticed in the south, albeit for different reasons: the economic crisis will fail because of the commercial activity of the fair, and crisis-woman will fail to be noticed because she is so thin and unappealing that, to put it in the crudest of terms, she will not be able to "sell" herself on the market down there.

While the two women are dressed in fashions that are similarly stylish, the crisis-woman is distinguished from the fuller-figured woman in several crucial ways. Her skeletal thinness shows in her taut jaw, her bony neck, her emaciated arms, and her slender waist that is accentuated by a thick black belt. Her figure also evokes a sense of bodily unease. Her head is turned so far to the right that it seems unnatural. The position of her left arm, which uncannily juts out from behind her back, suggests an uncomfortable flatness and two-dimensionality. The *donna-crisi* holds a glove in her left hand that limply hangs down and suggests the weakness of her body. The bangle on her left arm is a measure of her thinness, and the purse she holds draws attention to her material concerns.[41] Her fuller-figured counterpart instead has a voluptuous flowing shawl to evoke her presumed sexuality and fecundity which is further echoed in the billowing breast-shaped sails of the ship on the poster behind her.

But if these two women are markedly different, they are also strikingly similar: they both wear beret hats; the cut of their dress is the same; the neckline of each dress is fringed in white lace; and their hair is similarly styled. Elements of each are clearly recognizable in the other. One might suggest that the crisis-woman reads just as much as an uncanny double of the fuller-figured woman as she does her pathetic imitation.[42] Such similarity might be troubling from a fascist point of view, especially given the notable lack of other distinctive features that often characterize the crisis-woman. For example, if fascist dictates argue that part of the crisis-woman's threat lay in her foreign origin, nowhere in the cartoon is this apparent. Nothing marks the crisis-woman as less Italian than her fuller-figured counterpart. Neither is the crisis woman especially "masculinized" as fascist dictates would have it (aside, of course, from her thin form). Also missing are overt references to the demographic campaign, to eugenics, or to social hygiene. Rather than stressing the elements of fascist dictates to the Italian press, d'Angara's illustration – like other satirical cartoons – works to subtly interpellate the reader through the mechanism of laughter.

What is there to laugh about here from a fascist point of view given such similarities? The key to laughter lies, once again, in one's ability or inability to decode a given set of signs. Although the crisis-woman attempts to make herself attractive by wearing clothes that are equally as fashionable as the fuller-figured woman, she is unconscious of the most obvious obstacle to her desirability: her excessively thin body. In short, the sign that she misreads is her own body. This mistake sums up the fundamental flaw of the crisis-woman as she is represented here and elsewhere: *she fails read her body as a sign*. The reader and the fuller-figured woman understand very well the implications of her silhouette, and with that knowledge are positioned to mock the crisis-woman's intentions of finding a man at the fair.

Underlying d'Angara's cartoon is a suggestion that many of these cartoons share: the female body is nothing less than a system of signs that when aligned with fascist ideals reads as desirable, and when misaligned reads as repellent. These signs "code" the female body, as Foucault would put it, by classifying and taxonomizing it. This classification, obviously, dovetails with fascist bodily ideals: the body is either that of a subject or an object; it is appealing or repulsive; it belongs to a crisis-woman or to a wholesome woman. In each of these texts, the signs presented by the body of the crisis-woman construct a normative knowledge and "truth" about women's bodies, a knowledge that fulfils this satire's ameliorative pedagogical aims: the female body is beautiful only when it is rotund and curvaceous.[43] These texts repeatedly assure the reader – whether male or female – that the crisis-woman is pathetically ridiculous and is neither a figure to be emulated nor one to desire.

The Crisis-Woman in the Colonial Context: Abjection and the Female Body

In the previous two chapters, I have traced the contours of the palpable "threat to the race" that the anti-demographic crisis-woman represented in fascist ideology. Given this background, it will not come as a surprise to find that some of the most pointed images of the crisis-woman's abjection are to be found in cartoons set in the colonial context, which place this female figure alongside typified racialized depictions of the African Other. I present two examples here, the first of which is Mameli Barbara's cartoon entitled "Non-utilitarian Crisis-Woman" ["Donna crisi inutilitaria"] (Figure 11; captions in Appendix D). The reader will quickly recognize this drawing as a complement to the previously discussed "Utilitarian Crisis-Woman" by the same artist. "Non-utilitarian Crisis-Woman," however, contains a sequence of images that tell the story of a *donna-crisi* who is captured by a group of cannibals on African terrain. When the cannibals bring her to their curvaceous, semi-nude African queen, she rejects the catch and angrily cries: "The Lenten fast is over. What can I get off this bone?" [La quaresima è passata. Cosa spolpo, da quest'osso?]. The crisis-woman, it would seem, makes a better flagpole than meal. The second cartoon is Paolo Garretto's untitled illustration showing a crisis-woman tied to a stake while two African cannibals, who look more like gorillas than human beings, regard their captive with interest (Figure 12). One African is apparently intended to be royalty and, in addition to a grass skirt, wears an eclectic collection of clothing presumably gleaned from his former victims: a top hat, a crown, and a boot on one foot. His servant, apparently a cook, wears a white apron and has hung a rather large butcher knife in its string. The crisis-woman looks on, with dispassionate interest, as the cook measures her thin arm between his thick fingers. "They must have already eaten her, your Majesty," he says, "There's not even enough here to make an osso buco" [La devono aver già mangiata, Maestà! Non c'è nemmeno di che farci un osso buco].

Both of these cartoons are notable insofar as they imagine scenes of a deferred cannibalism, a fantasy that says as much about the representation of the crisis-woman as the African.[44] Cannibalism raises the question of proper uses of the body, and here the African and the crisis-woman are aligned by their perverse misuse of the body: the first ingests what should not be ingested and the second fails to ingest what should.[45] But more than misuse of the body, Barbara's cartoon in particular aligns two types of deviant, pathological sexuality: the androgynous, desexed crisis-woman and her opposite, the curvaceous, hungry African queen – otherwise recognizable as that widespread caricature of nineteenth- and early-twentieth-century black femininity, the Hottentot Venus.

Sander Gilman, in *Difference and Pathology,* presents a useful genealogy of the Hottentot Venus within the context of a larger discussion of influential nineteenth-century images of black sexuality. He focuses in

Figure 11. "Donna crisi inutilitaria" ["Non-utilitarian crisis-woman"]. By Mameli Barbara for *Marc'Aurelio* (19 April 1933). See Appendix D for captions. (By permission of the Ministero dei beni e delle attività culturali e del turismo della Repubblica Italiana/Biblioteca Nazionale Centrale di Firenze. Reproduction prohibited.)

particular on significant medical and anthropological texts, such as Cesare Lombroso's *La donna delinquente*, and shows how the black African woman was perceived by scientists as the "lowest exemplum of mankind on the great chain of being."[46] She was viewed as the "epitome" of "sexual lasciviousness" and was linked to other degenerate

— *La devono aver già mangiata, Maestà! Non c'è nemmeno di che farci un osso buco.*

Figure 12. Untitled, Paolo Garretto, 1933. Published in a pamphlet entitled *Donne crisi.* The caption reads: "They must have already eaten her, your Majesty! There's not even enough here to make an osso buco." (By permission of the Ministero dei beni e delle attività culturali e del turismo della Repubblica Italiana/Biblioteca Nazionale Centrale di Firenze. Reproduction prohibited.)

figures such as the syphilitic, the lesbian, and the prostitute.[47] The telltale signs of this primitive, degenerate – or as Lombroso would say, "atavistic" – concupiscence were evident in the Hottentot's physique: nineteenth-century medical inquiry argued that she had deformed genitalia and suffered from steatopygia, or protruding buttocks. As Gilman points out, the fascination with the buttocks can be understood simply as a displacement for the fascination with the genitalia: "When the nineteenth century saw the black female, it saw her in terms of her buttocks, and saw represented by the buttocks all the anomalies of her genitalia."[48] Barbara's depiction of the African queen shows this same displaced interest in the genitalia; however, rather than exaggerated buttocks the queen has exaggerated breasts with erect nipples, a rounded belly, and especially curvaceous legs. The most notable feature of her headdress is the two diabolical-looking horns, and at her waist she wears a belt of phallic-shaped objects that resemble bananas. Her appetite for "white flesh" can easily be read as an extension of her well-known perverse sexual appetite.

Although the crisis-woman – the figure opposed to the African queen – is white, she does not serve as a contrasting positive model of sexuality.[49] She is instead a contrasting yet equally degenerate model of female sexuality. Mameli draws here on a familiar representational convention that parallels black and white sexual deviance.[50] Not only does the crisis-woman *have* no appetite, but she can also *stimulate* no appetite – even in the most lascivious of creatures, let alone in the healthy white male. Her thin and physically weak body, which makes her a "substandard plunder" [bottino scadente] according to the captions, can only reflect a similar deformity in her sexual organs.

But these cartoons at the same time align and distinguish the cannibal and the crisis-woman. Both propose that the *donna-crisi* is so abject that even the cannibal does not desire her. If the anthropophagic violence against her body is deferred since she does not have enough flesh on her bones to make a meal – even one such as *osso buco* – there is another type of violence that has already seemingly been carried out: the violence that the crisis-woman has perpetrated against her own body, of excessive thinness. The signs of this violence are initially unreadable to the cannibals since they have assumed, in capturing her, that the crisis woman is as edible as any other white person. Upon closer inspection, however, even the cannibals are able to see that the crisis-woman is different from other whites they have presumably captured in the past. She is rejected even by "savages" and cannot be classed with other "civilized" persons of her race.[51] In sum, she is so abject as to be inhuman. She falls into no culturally intelligible category of being or, as Butler puts it, she inhabits an "'uninhabitable' zone of social life." Indeed, she seems already to be dead since the cannibal in Garretto's cartoon assumes she has already been eaten.

"Curing" the Crisis-Woman: "Therapeutic" Sexual Violence

In 1933 the smash-hit "Mah, cos'è questa crisi?" by Rodolfo De Angelis finally prescribed a reliable cure for the crisis-woman. In his song, De Angelis says to the crisis-woman: "Eat a bunch of potatoes, don't waste my nights, and you'll see that the curves will return!" [Mangi un sacco di patate, non mi sprechi le nottate e vedrà che la curva tornerà!] (see Appendix A for lyrics).[52] De Angelis's dual remedy of gastronomic consumption ("eat a bunch of potatoes") and sexual consummation ("don't waste my nights") makes explicit the ways in which the former is often a metaphor for the latter in satirical representations of the crisis-woman. Indeed, as we have just seen, the cannibal's appetite for white flesh functions in exactly the same way insofar as it points to a perverse sexual appetite of uncontrollable excess. The crisis-woman, however, is distinguished not by an excess but by a lack of appetite, in both the gastronomic and sexual senses.

This dual remedy of consumption-consummation is also proposed by Balzani, in his aforementioned song "Donna crisi."[53] Balzani advises his love not only to stop her dieting but to give herself over to him. He explains that her problem is not only that she doesn't want to satisfy *her own* appetite for food – "My Nina, I know what you eat for breakfast and lunch, a slice of lemon with three apples *alla giudìa*" [Tu pe' pranzo e colazione so che magni, Nina mia, una coccia de limone co' tre mele alla giudìa] – but also, more importantly, that she doesn't want to satisfy *his* sexual appetite:

> You go to soccer games, to dog races,
> you practice sports perfectly, you play the piano for four hands …
> but you never have a spare minute for lovemaking!
> My heart says that if I marry you – "My Nina, this is the problem!" –
> to have kids and be happy … I'll have to buy an incubator!
>
> Vai ar mècce der pallone, a le corse de li cani
> fai lo sport a perfezione, sòni er piano a quattro mani …
> ma però pe' fà l'amore nun ciài mai un minuto spiccio!

Si te sposo dice er core: "Nina mia, sta qui l'impiccio!":
perché p'avé li fiji e esse felice ... me toccherà comprà l'incubatrice!

That Balzani may need to buy an incubator to have a child with Nina seems more a result of the fact that she "never has a spare minute for lovemaking" rather than the unmentioned (and seemingly more obvious) possibility that she is thin and consequently sterile. Nevertheless, at a certain point, the exasperated singer calls out: "Oy! I'm sick of gnawing on a bone!" [ahò! me so stufato a rosicamme l'ossa!]. The crisis-woman's lack of appetite points to her pathological lack of sexual responsiveness and, as both Balzani and De Angelis suggest, curing one will cure the other.[54]

Balzani's song functions through many of the same tropes of objectification as those presented in satirical cartoons, and he clearly draws a large part of his material from these visual sources. His thin lover is not like the "steak filet" [bistecca ar' filoncino], to which the singer advises her to aspire, but like a scant bone or a "candle wick" ['no stoppino]. To satisfy a man like himself, he explains, "one needs a woman made like a sandwich" [ce vò 'na donna fatta a pagnottella]. His desire to sexually consume the crisis-woman, as evidenced by the gastronomic metaphors he uses here, takes us back to the question of violence raised in the previous section on cannibalism.

Unlike the cannibal, however, Balzani and De Angelis do not reject the crisis-woman; conforming to the didactic aims that characterize satirical texts, they propose to cure her, or as Balzani generously puts it, "Since I like you, I want to give you some advice" [Siccome tu me piaci e io un conzijo te vojo dà]. For both Balzani and De Angelis, to "cure" the crisis-woman is to sexually violate her, and in doing so to transform her sexuality from deviant to normalized. Especially in Balzani's song, one can clearly see how his desires directly oppose hers. Nina, the modern woman, is so busy with her own leisure activities – some of them, such as soccer games and dog races, notably coded as masculine – that she cannot be bothered with Balzani's need for lovemaking. Although she is interested in neither consumption nor consummation, Balzani's advice is that they would be therapeutic, *even if they go against her wishes*. The violation Balzani and De Angelis propose produces a recognizable sexual norm, which we have seen throughout the previous chapters, that equates healthy female sexuality with submission, violation, and victimization rather than that modelled by the incredible but inedible Nina.

Forced and Subversive Laughter

As I have shown throughout this chapter, each of these cartoons provokes a type of laughter that harmonizes with hegemonic fascist social and cultural mores, and one must understand these texts as part of a larger machinery of fascist propaganda. Despite this machinery, however, one wonders if these texts might also have provoked another type of laughter in addition to the hegemonic – a type that went against the grain of fascist values and ideals.

To recognize that these texts are part of a larger machinery of fascist propaganda is to remember that behind Polverelli's dictates inciting the press to disparage the crisis-woman lay a very real threat for the directors, writers, and artists of the *giornali satirici e umoristici*: the threat of closure, heavy fines, and imprisonment. As historian Paolo Murialdi points out in his book *La stampa del regime*, from the early 1920s forward Mussolini increasingly restricted the freedom of the Italian press in an attempt to control it.[55] Two royal decrees – the first passed in July 1923 and the second in July 1924 – were important antecedents to the now infamous 1925 *Legge sulla stampa*, which definitively concentrated power in the hands of a few directors of state-approved publications rather than dispersing it at the grass-roots journalistic or editorial level.[56] This law ensured that all sectors of the press apparatus were restructured and integrated into newer organizations with direct connections to the fascist corporate state. Finally, and most frighteningly, the tough reforms of the 1930 Rocco Penal Code drastically increased the number of crimes that one might commit through the apparatus of the press, as well as the consequences for committing them. According to the earlier Zanardelli penal code, crimes that were committed through the apparatus of the press – such as offending the king or government – held a punishment of six months' imprisonment or a fine of one hundred to two thousand lire.[57] The Rocco Penal Code introduced the following:

> Those who should publicly offend the Crown, the government of the King, the Fascist Grand Council or the Parliament, or only one of the two Chambers, shall be punished with imprisonment from *one to six years*. The same penalty applies to those who should publicly offend the Armed Forces of the State or judicial order.[58]

Given the obvious breadth with which these rules could be interpreted, it is not surprising to discover that a publication like *Marc'Aurelio* "was sequestered several times until, with the passing of the years, it completely conformed to the regime."[59] Thus, although the laughter provoked by the cartoons I have been describing supports fascist ideals, the stimulus for that laughter was also, to a certain extent, clearly forced.

But the cartoons of the *giornali satirici ed umoristici* may also arguably raise the possibility of subversive laughter that resists fascist mores, since it is precisely this type of publication that has historically directed criticisms against governmental policies and politics. One is compelled to ask if there was not room for the release of subtly coded, subversive laughter that might have escaped the keen eyes of fascist censors and thus undermined hegemonic culture celebrating the robust rural and prolific woman. If laughter builds consensus, and works as a social rite, then it can also work in the opposite way, as an anti-rite – albeit with great difficulty in an authoritarian state. Samuel Weber, for one, speaks of the "ambivalent character of laughter" and argues that in the classical tradition it is "dangerous to the guardians of the state ... because of its tendency to get out of hand."[60] Freud, too, argues that certain jokes, namely hostile or tendentious jokes, are often used against those in authority.

In order to further explore this possibility, let us look at a special article, published by *Marc'Aurelio,* that was intended to launch their campaign against the *donna-crisi.* On 15 March 1933 a front-page editorial proclaimed: "It's Time to Tell All About the Crisis Type of Woman!!" [È ora di dire tutto sulla donna tipo crisi!!]. The editorial explains the importance and meaning of cartoons that mock the crisis-woman, which *Marc'Aurelio* is about to begin publishing at this point almost weekly. It opens by asking a few rhetorical questions: "What does one really mean by 'crisis type of woman'? Does she bring bad luck? What charming features does she possess?", and states, "To this and other questions we propose to give an answer in the following article" [Che cosa s'intende propriamente per donna tipo crisi? È essa apportatrice di jettatura? Quali attrattive può possedere la donna crisi? A queste e ad altre domande ci proponiamo di dare una risposta nel seguente articolo].[61] The answers to these pressing questions are laid out for the reader right away:

> First of all, by crisis type of woman one refers to that certain type of woman to whom nature gives heaviness and thinness in proportions permitted by its law, but who is affected by a degenerate aesthetic sense, by a certain amount of progressive stupidity, and by literary snobbism, and who submits herself to a series of therapies designed to reduce her to skin and bones. This type of woman is one of the most powerful vehicles of bad luck.

> Anzitutto, s'intende per donna tipo crisi, quel tale tipo di donna dotata da natura di grasso e magro in proporzioni permesse dalla legge, ma che affetta da un degenerato senso estetico, da una certa dose di stupidaggine progressiva e da snobismo letteratoso [sic], si sottopone ad una serie di cure atte a ridursi alla parte ossea. Questo tipo di donna è uno dei più potenti veicoli di jettatura.[62]

The article goes on to give several examples of the type of bad luck the crisis-woman brings: "If a tram stops because the electricity has gone out, look around and you will discover a crisis type of woman perched on her twiggy little legs" [Se il *tram* si ferma per mancanza di corrente guardatevi intorno e scoprirete appollaiata con le sue gambette stecchite la donna tipo crisi].[63] The article continues in this vein, and attributes an almost mystical power to the *donna-crisi*: "If the lights go out in the movie theatre or the reel breaks at the most interesting moment, you can be sure that there is a crisis type of woman in the hall" [Se si spegne la luce nel cinematografo o si rompe la pellicola nel momento più interessante, state pur certi che vi è una donna tipo crisi nella sala].[64] The crisis woman never laughs, she provokes morbid thoughts in others, and she encourages one to think thoughts that "the law of good manners and morals does not permit one to describe" [la legge sul buon costume e sulla morale non permette di descrivere].[65] This front-page editorial is reinforced by a cartoon that follows a few pages later: "Chiodo scaccia chiodo" (perhaps best translated as "One thing leads to another") by Attalo (the pen name of Gioachino Colizzi). A husband and a crisis-wife are walking down the street. Two men observe them from afar. "Do you see that man?" the first observer asks, and continues, "He married well in order to set himself up, and failed." [Vedi quello? Ha fatto un matrimonio d'interesse per sistemarsi, ed è fallito]. The second observer responds: "I've always said that the crisis-woman brings bad luck" [L'ho sempre detto io che la donna crisi porta jella].

Although one might take this editorial seriously, it also begs to be read in a satirical fashion. After all, it *is* published in *Marc'Aurelio*. Because its humour works through the juxtaposition of a grave tone with light-hearted material, one might read it as a tongue-in-cheek parody of fascist propaganda. This text works as a facetious comic text because it parodies the all-too-serious fascist subtext, examples of which abound in the previous two chapters of this book. Rather than pointing to the grave threat the crisis-woman poses to women's health and to the health of the nation, rather than speaking technically of "the repercussion of forced weight-loss upon fecundity and demographic efficiency," and rather than speaking loftily of "the greatest moral forces of fascist civilization" that she undermines, this article singles out the crisis-woman because she brings bad luck, because she can make a tram stop or a movie reel break, and because if you marry her for her wealth you will surely not get it. If the goal of this editorial is to provide an initial framework for reading the cartoons that *Marc'Aurelio* is about to start publishing on a regular basis, then it is significant that the humour here pokes fun at the bombast of fascist rhetoric. Although one can laugh at the crisis-woman and her "twiggy little legs" and her "progressive stupidity," one can *also* laugh at the ways in which fascist rhetoric is almost in and of itself absurdist. But we should remember that we are dealing with the cultural production of the "jokers" rather than the "rebels" here, to once again use Claudio Carabba's terminology. The political satire described here is subtle enough to keep under the radar and not draw attention to itself.

In regard to subversive humour, one might also observe that some cartoons that are purportedly about the *donna-crisi* also poke fun at other subjects – especially men who marry the crisis-woman. This change of target, even though it is often still in line with fascist mores, might have given female readers a chance to laugh at the follies of the opposite sex.[66] For example, the cartoon entitled "La moglie crisi" ["The crisis wife"], by Cesare Gobbo, shows a man with a cane in hand walking along a country road (Figure 13). He has turned to a telegraph pole on the side of the street and says, "Come out, silly woman! Do you think I haven't figured out that you've hidden behind that telegraph pole?" [Esci fuori mattacchiona! Credi che non l'ho capita che ti sei nascosta dietro il palo del telegrafo?]. Although this cartoon is clearly intended to make fun of the excessive thinness of the crisis-woman, the butt of the joke is arguably also the husband. His facial features are simplistic. His nose is excessively round and large. His hat and jacket look at bit worse for the wear and both are too small. At first sight, he seems to be a simpleton who is talking to an inanimate object. Indeed, the epithet that he applies to his wife ("silly" or "mad" [mattacchiona]) could just as easily be applied, in the masculine form, to himself. In my earlier discussion of objectification of the crisis-woman, I stress that if these cartoons are to retain their humour, then the crisis-woman can only *embody the qualities* of various long and slender objects, but she can never *actually be* those objects. This particular cartoon is a good illustration of what happens when there is no visible distinction between the

Figure 13. "La moglie crisi" ["The Crisis Wife"] by Cesare Gobbo for *Il Settebello* (22 November 1933). The caption reads: "Come out, silly woman! Do you think I haven't figured out that you've hidden behind that telegraph pole?" (By permission of the Ministero dei beni e delle attività culturali e del turismo della Repubblica Italiana/Biblioteca Nazionale Centrale di Firenze. Reproduction prohibited.)

crisis-woman and the object to which she is compared. The result is that the humour is redirected away from the negative figure of the crisis-woman and towards other targets, in this case, the husband. On a related but slightly different note, we might return to ambiguous male figures such as the husband in "Amuleti" ["Lucky Charms"], who seems a bit too foppish and a bit too much of a dandy. He is certainly not a paragon of male virility based on the Mussolinian model, and his bourgeois self-absorption could just as easily be the target of laughter as his wife's excessively slim body. Thus, many of these images might be read in multiple ways while at the same time they clearly advance hegemonic ideals about thinness and femininity.

Finally, one might argue that although these cartoons position the reader to laugh in agreement with fascist ideals, this positioning does not seamlessly coincide with the ideological dictates of governmental institutions in the same way as an article in a fashion magazine or medical journal might. While aesthetic guidelines for fashion were set down by the Ente Nazionale della Moda (ENM) from the 1930s forward, and demographic initiatives directed at women were overseen by organizations such as the ONMI or governmental bodies such as the Demorazza (as the Office for Demography and Race was commonly called), there was no such body overseeing Italian humour. Although satirical cartoons are certainly governed by political power through the Ufficio Stampa and later the Minculpop, both of which regulated the press, these institutions regulated *all* types of publications, from the daily news to fashion magazines to official publications. This being said, however, a broader fascist discursive system that emphasized compliance to the regime at every level cannot be denied, and it is to this discursive regime that we once again turn in the next chapter.

4

Ideologies and Economies of Crisis

Thus far I have presented the *donna-crisi* primarily as a figure that is symptomatic of a variety of historical shifts and of fascism's response to them. For example, aversion to the crisis-woman's lack of feminine attributes can be read as a displaced fear of changing gender roles that accompanied Italy's interwar process of modernization. Criticism of her indecorous use of makeup and fashionable clothing might reflect the manner in which the rise of consumer culture provoked anxieties about the erasure of traditional class markers. Unease about her exotic taste could show concern about foreign influence upon Italy, particularly the influence of models of femininity conveyed via the French fashion and American film industries. Condemnation of her sterility might be seen as a sign of anxiety about the rapid growth of urban populations or the so-called decline of the race. Finally, the crisis-woman was a figure that raised concerns about women's work, women's sports, and generally speaking women's entrance into the public sphere. While such a historical and symptomatic reading is extremely important, below I argue that in order to arrive at a fuller understanding of the *donna-crisi*, this type of reading must be joined with a discursive and ideological one.

This chapter builds on the work of scholars like Barbara Spackman who give serious and sustained consideration to the ideological formations of fascism.[1] I begin this chapter by reading the *donna-crisi* as a figure of ideological fantasy, drawing on the work of Slavoj Žižek and tracing the discursive mechanisms that generate meaning about her. This discussion of the crisis-woman provides a springboard to a broader discussion of the ways in which the regime attempted to realize its goals by strategically manufacturing and deploying the notion of crisis.

Throughout this chapter I will refer back to the cultural artefacts discussed above – both as concrete touchstones that illustrate an abstract theoretical point and as points of connection between this chapter and preceding ones.

An Ideological Reading of the Crisis-Woman

As a figure of propaganda designed to simultaneously proscribe women's identification with modern female types and incite them to make more babies, the *donna-crisi* might be considered a fascist ideological figure *par excellence*. As I have shown earlier, fascist logic maintained that women who were even vaguely interested in ideas, thoughts, or behaviours that could be termed "modern" risked becoming the abject crisis-woman unless they engaged in a precise scrutiny of their all-too-corruptible female body. According to this logic, however, there is an intriguing and potentially disruptive contiguity between the undesirable crisis-woman and other, more popular types of modern women. When one looks at the variegated landscape of 1930s Italian popular culture to which the crisis-woman belongs – a culture characterized by the proliferation of non-hegemonic female types in advertisements, glossy magazines, films, pulp novels, and commodity culture in general – one cannot help but wonder if the crisis-woman was a figure that worked in more complex ways than those suggested by her propagandistic intent. In other words, could this modern female figure – who was unabashedly cosmopolitan and more attentive to the latest exotic Parisian fashions than to the prosaic duties of motherhood – have been understood as symbolizing opposition to fascist ideals rather than as simply reinforcing them? Does the abject representation of the modern woman have any commonalities with other, more desirable representations of the modern woman? If there are commonalities, to what extent if any might the crisis-woman be read as a figure of resistance to fascist ideals?

There are two main types of response to this set of questions. The first is essentially historical: one might consider the extent to which the fascist regime had an ideological grip on its subjects, that is, the extent to which women as lived historical subjects believed in the threat represented by the crisis-woman. The second path is ideological: one might consider the discursive mechanisms that generate meaning about the crisis-woman within the larger framework of fascist ideology, and ask if and how this negative figure points to the potential internal contradictions or conflicts of that framework.

Before I embark on an ideological reading, let me first outline the historical response to this question. A logical place to begin would be to call attention to the antagonistic split between the lofty fascist vision of woman as prolific mother and the daily habits (as well as the material needs) of women living under the fascist regime. This split is well documented by historians. De Grazia, for example, points out that women's role in the workforce necessarily evolved with Italy's increasing modernization (which was ironically spurred on by the same regime that wanted to keep women at home and away from work):

> as agriculture's weight in the national economy declined with respect to that of industry, women fled from back-breaking rural enterprise. As the tertiary sector boomed in the twentieth century, office work became more and more feminized. As manufacture shifted from producer to consumer goods, women workers moved from the declining textiles and other light manufacture ... to the mechanized heavy and consumer-goods production typical of advanced industrialism.[2]

Within the field of education, Alexander De Grand notes that women's university enrolments grew throughout the twenty black years and that as more women received degrees in higher education their ideas became more emancipated. De Grand shows how even the official publication of the fascist women's auxiliary, *Il giornale della donna*, advanced politically questionable ideals when it "began a page for university women, [which] promptly became a sounding board for heterogeneous opinions" that ranged from protests "against the limitations against women in state examinations" to paying homage "to the female student" rather than the mother "as the true hero for persevering in the face of tremendous obstacles."[3] With regard to the general impact of fascist propaganda upon women, Lesley Caldwell points out "the negligible results that this barrage of initiatives [directed at women and the family] appears to have had in concrete terms."[4] Moreover, she observes that the "personal significance [of this propaganda] for the masses of Italian women" at the level of lived experience is complex and contradictory, or in her words "another dimension altogether."[5] The oral histories of Turin's working class collected by Luisa Passerini support Caldwell's assertion that women responded in varying ways to fascist initiatives. With regard to the demographic campaign, Passerini states that "even those [interviewees] who previously expressed a certain sympathy for the Duce display implacable opposition on this issue."[6] Passerini interviews women who not only recall limiting the number of children they had, but who also illegally shared information about contraception and even clandestinely carried out their own home abortions – despite the health and legal risks of such a procedure. Gigliola Gori bluntly states: "Clearly, Mussolini's notion that producing more than four children was the best way in which a woman could defeat infant mortality and other 'negative factors' failed to convince many women."[7]

The historical narratives cited above have in common the same fundamental question: to what extent did fascist ideology really take hold of women living under the regime? Or, put slightly differently, to what extent did women consent to pronatalist ideals and to what extent did they resist them? If women did not unconditionally buy into the values of the regime, as this historiography suggests, then there is certainly room to make a strong argument that women might have felt a critical distance between their own lives and propagandistic exempla such as the *donna-madre*. Correspondingly, they might have felt a certain allegiance with supposedly negative figures like the *donna-crisi*. But one can go only so far in a historical analysis that focuses on the nature of consent and resistance. Given the types of primary sources available, any further assumptions about how women viewed figures such as the *donna-madre* and the *donna-crisi* would be mere speculation.

If, however, we shift paradigms and focus on the discursive mechanisms through which representations of the *donna-crisi* operate, we can come up with another, perhaps more productive, reading: the crisis-woman is a multivalent figure that belongs to a nexus of fascist ideological fantasies in which the corporeal, the modern, and the national interlock. She supports several fantasies that were crucial to fascist ideology: first, the reproductive fantasy that an increase in Italy's population would lead to an increase in political power on the world stage; second, the fantasy of authoritarian modernization, which suggested that modernization could take place on exclusively fascist terms, uncontaminated by other concurrent models such as American-style consumer culture; and third, the fantasy of society as a unified whole, which cast fascism as a political force able to bind the nation together as a entity whose integrity was unaffected by regional, class, linguistic, or other differences.[8] But, as I shall shortly show, the crisis-woman is also a figure that points to the untenability of these fantasies – and it is perhaps in this sense that we might read her as an oppositional figure, that is, a figure that simultaneously points to not only the dream but the failure of fascist ideals.

In order to unpack this assertion, it is necessary to take a detour through the work of Slavoj Žižek, upon which it is based. Let us begin with the claim that the crisis-woman is a product of ideological fantasy. In *The Sublime Object of Ideology,* Žižek outlines the workings of ideological fantasy and distinguishes this concept from the workings of ideology as it has traditionally been conceived. While the established Marxist notion of ideology posits "a divergence between so-called social reality and our distorted representation, our false consciousness of it,"[9] Žižek on the other hand argues that "the fundamental level of ideology is not of an illusion masking the real state of things but that of an (unconscious) fantasy structuring our social reality itself."[10] The basic Marxist formula of ideology is, "They do not know it, but they are doing it."[11] Žižek reformulates Marx and says instead, "They know very well how things really are, but they are still doing it as if they did not know."[12] To give an example relevant to the context of fascist Italy, consider the crisis-woman's frequent pairing with the prolific mother, illustrated for example in the drawing "Cocktail" (Figure 4). We might observe that although people knew very well that figures like the *donna-madre* and *donna-crisi* did not represent the realities of women's lives, they continued to treat them as if they did; they continued to invest these figures with desire or disgust, as the case may be, and in doing so imbued them with power and authenticity.

Looking more closely at Žižek's model in comparison to the Marxist one, we see that "the illusion is not on the side of knowledge, it is already on the side of reality itself, of what the people are doing."[13] Žižek observes: "The illusion is therefore double: it consists in overlooking the illusion which is structuring our real, effective relationship to reality. And this overlooked, unconscious illusion is what may be called the *ideological fantasy.*"[14] Returning to the example of the crisis-woman, we can say that the overlooked unconscious illusion embedded in social reality is the fact that although the threat of the *donna-crisi* is completely imaginary, people nonetheless acted as if it were real. They acted as if the demographic crisis would be eased if women stopped following fashion trends that encouraged them to become like the dangerous crisis-woman. They acted as if eliminating the crisis-woman would eliminate other non-fascist models of modern femininity. They acted as if ridding the country of antagonistic figures like the crisis-woman would lead to the realization of a racially pure and unified fascist state. The publications on the crisis-woman that I discuss in chapter 1, ranging from the overtly fascist *Giornale della donna* to the more cosmopolitan *Amica,* illustrate very well this illusion.

As a product of ideological fantasy much like that of the African or the Jew, the crisis-woman is a symbolically overdetermined figure that stands for pure difference, for radical exteriority and otherness. As we saw in chapter 2, she condenses a wide variety of threats: bourgeois decadence, egoism, individualism, debauched morals, sexual promiscuity, the perversion of sex roles, social upheaval, consumer culture, mass culture, urbanism, anti-naturalism, foreign corruption, physical degeneration, racial degeneration, and the collapse of the nation. It is through this process of condensation that the figure of the crisis-woman acquires meaning. These threats function through a discursive "chain of equivalence," to use Laclau and Mouffe's terminology, according to which each invokes the other.[15] That is, to talk about the crisis-woman's egoism is to talk about her debauched morals. To talk about her debauched morals is to talk about the perversion of sex roles, and so on. Each element in this chain is not a distinct element; rather, its identity is established by that which it has in common with other elements – namely, sheer negativity.

In addition to this condensation, the crisis-woman is a figure onto which the traumatic antagonisms of modern Italian society could be displaced. She was a figure that permitted the fascist regime to account for the split between its vision of a unified social body and the realities of a society divided, say, along class lines. Rather than acknowledging the possibility that middle-class or bourgeois women saw the fecund *donna-madre* as undesirable because she seemed peasant-like and lower class, fascism blamed their rejection of the prolific mother on the *donna-crisi* – a foreign model of femininity that seduced women into adopting a misguided set of values and ideas about womanhood. The same logic could be used to explain other resistances, for example that of working-class women to demographic policy (illustrated in Passerini's interviews): it was, quite simply, the crisis-woman's fault.

What particularly sets Žižek's argument apart is that he does not simply argue that the figure of the Other is a locus for the condensation and displacement of already existing antagonisms in the social fabric but, perhaps more importantly, also maintains that the process (condensation and displacement) by which an ideological fantasy masks the antagonistic conflicts of a given society in fact "is a means for an ideology to take its own failure into account into advance."[16] The ideological construct of the Other is necessary for the fantasy. Žižek uses the figure of the Jew in Nazi Germany to illustrate his point, a useful example that helps us draw out the parallels to the figure of the crisis-woman: "Far from being the positive cause of social antagonism, the

'Jew' is just the embodiment of a certain blockage – of the impossibility which prevents the society from achieving its full identity as a closed, homogeneous totality ... Society is not prevented from achieving its full identity because of Jews: it is prevented by its own antagonistic nature, by its own immanent blockage, and it 'projects' this internal negativity into the figure of the 'Jew.'"[17] Thus the *donna-crisi* is a necessary figure for fascist ideology insofar as she accounts for the failure of fascist ideology to fully realize its goals, whether they are to make the Italian nation sixty million people strong, to modernize under exclusively authoritarian terms, or to bring Italians together into one national body. We can identify the crisis-woman as a transgressive figure not so much based on the extent to which women potentially identified with her but for the ways in which she threatens to expose the very impossibility of fascist ideological fantasy from within. Rather than viewing the crisis-woman as a potential figure of oppositional political identification, a figure through which lived historical subjects could express their opposition to the regime, we must read her as a multivalent figure that is both produced by and undermines fascist power.

Fascism's Economy of Crisis

In chapter 1 we saw how the *grande crisi*, or Great Depression, launched an Italian obsession with the notion of crisis, and how – thanks to Polverelli's dictates – the *donna-crisi* emerged as a negative figure of fascist propaganda precisely at this moment. We looked at several tongue-in-cheek articles from popular magazines of the era that illustrated Italy's "crisis" obsession. One article spoke of the hyperbolic use of the word "crisis" that "must be pronounced each time one alludes to any type of human activity."[18] Another mocked the overuse of the term, describing "a crisis because our shoes leak, because we've caught a cold, because we yawn at the theatre, because we don't digest cake."[19] At this point, I want to join this historical and cultural observation with a political and ideological one: that fascist discourse frequently turned on an economy of crisis that exhaustively asserted the primacy of crisis at all levels of culture.

We can begin to flesh out this assertion through the work of Chiara Ferrari. In her article on the discursive characteristics of the theme of ritual sacrifice in Mussolini's speeches, Ferrari makes the larger argument that crisis is a central component of fascist discourse. She maintains that the regime repeatedly justified its actions as a preventive measure against an imminent crisis: "the simultaneous displacement and reintroduction of ... crisis continued to characterize fascist rhetoric (albeit with various inflections and shifting definitions of what constituted the crisis), until the end of the regime."[20] A concrete example can be found in the rhetoric of the demographic campaign, which strategically emphasized – or in Ferrari's terms, displaced and reintroduced – various types of crises: the debacle of falling birth rates, the menacing increase of social disease in urban centres, and the risk that Italy might be reduced to a colony rather than develop into a commanding imperial force.

Taking Ferrari's analysis a step further, I would argue that one productive way to view the operations of fascist ideology is to explore the ways in which it functioned through an "economy of crisis."[21] I take this term from Jacques Derrida, who explains that "the 'representation' of crisis, and the rhetoric that it organizes, always have at the end this goal: to identify, in order to limit, a more serious and formless threat, in reality without shape and without norm ... By deeming it in crisis, one tames it, domesticates it, neutralizes it, in short one makes an economy out of it."[22] Let us once again take the demographic campaign as a case in point. As I will show in what follows, when the regime named the falling birth rate a demographic *crisis* and anxiously focused on the vigilant management of threats to the social body, in effect it attempted to tame a more shifting and nebulous threat, that of the invalidation of the totalitarian aspects of the fascist project itself.

In order to get a better sense of how an economy of crisis works within the larger framework of fascist ideology, let us turn to the writings of fascism's most iconic and vociferous representative, Benito Mussolini. On 26 May 1927 Mussolini spoke to the lower house of Parliament, giving what was to become one of his most well-remembered and well-studied speeches, the *Discorso dell'ascensione* or Ascension Day speech.[23] This lengthy speech officially launched fascism's demographic campaign whose pronatalist measures, as we know, were directed mainly at women.[24] With its obsession with population decline and recurrent vivid imagery of a nation on the brink of death, the Ascension Day speech is an excellent example of fascism's economy of crisis.

Mussolini sets the stage for crisis by using the metaphor of a doctor examining a gravely ill patient: he states that the first part of his address consists of an "examination of the situation of the Italian population from the viewpoint of physical and racial well-being" [esame della situazione del popolo italiano dal punto di vista della salute fisica e della razza].[25] Soon afterward he casts himself in the role of the physician: "I am the doctor who does not overlook the symptoms" [Io sono il medico che non trascura i sintomi].[26] The "situation" of the Italian population, as one might imagine, is dire; the nation is in critical condition and "the picture ... is rather grim" [il quadro ... è abbastanza grigio].[27] Italy suffers from a wide variety of "so-called social diseases" [malattie cosiddette sociali], all of which are on the rise: pellagra, tuberculosis, malignant tumours, malaria, alcoholism, mental illness, and suicides.[28] Most importantly, however – and, Mussolini repeatedly stresses, contrary to commonplace opinion – Italy's population is rapidly and perilously declining along with that of other European countries.

The recurrent imagery of disease and imminent death in the Ascension Day speech localizes the symptoms of an alarming population crisis in the body. The Duce's solution to Italy's demographic decline likewise focuses on the body. He will not act like past Liberal leaders whose *modus operandi* was "let things be, let things happen" [lasciar fare, lasciar correre], which he calls a "suicidal theory" [teoria suicida].[29] Instead, the dictator recommends immediate intervention since the "treatment of the physical health of the population must be of primary importance" [la cura della salute fisica del popolo deve essere al primo posto].[30] "It's a fact," he later says, "that the destiny of nations is linked to their demographic power" [sta di fatto che il destino delle nazioni è legato alla loro potenza demografica].[31] Mussolini's cure – summed up in the slogan "maximum natality and minimum mortality" [massimo di natalità, minimo di mortalità] – is to increase Italy's population to sixty million by mid-century.[32] This would be achieved through the workings of the Opera Nazionale per la Maternità ed Infanzia as well as the establishment of "healthy" non-urban industries in Italy, and it would be financed through new taxes like the celibacy tax and perhaps even a tax on "infertile" marriages.[33]

When examining this speech, one immediately notices that its motor, the force that drives it, is an imminent sense of crisis. Moreover, the construction of this crisis is pointedly tactical. Mussolini *deploys* the idea of crisis precisely in order to *create* a threat and then *neutralize* it, thereby proclaiming victory over it. Mussolini concludes his address with a triumphant prediction of Italy's transformation under fascist rule. Currently a nation on the brink of collapse, Italy shall become a nation with completely new features: "Today we are forewarning the world of the creation of a powerful, unified Italian State, from the Alps to Sicily ... Only I can tell you that, in ten years time, Italy, our Italy, will be unrecognizable to herself and to foreigners because we will have radically transformed her features, and most of all her spirit" [Oggi preannunziamo al mondo la creazione del potente Stato unitario italiano, dalle Alpi alla Sicilia ... Solo io vi dico che, tra dieci anni, l'Italia, la nostra Italia, sarà irriconoscibile a se stessa ed agli stranieri, perché noi l'avremo trasformata radicalmente nel suo volto, ma soprattutto nella sua anima].[34] Two points must be underscored here. First, the crisis situation that Mussolini touts is highly manufactured insofar as the Duce presents a skewed picture of recent changes in Italy's population. Although Italy's birth rate certainly was declining, this did not result in a decrease in the overall population, since the nation's death rate was also down. In fact, the overall population was experiencing steady growth.[35] Second, not only is the crisis of which Mussolini speaks manufactured but so are the purported effects of his "cure." In his examination of the success of the demographic campaign, historian Massimo Livi-Bacci draws the conclusion that "the direct long-range effects of the fascist demographic policy seem to have been very modest, if any existed at all."[36]

What I find especially interesting about this unusually long-winded speech – which is understood by historians and cultural scholars alike as a speech that kicked off the demographic campaign – is the fact that Mussolini rather quickly abandons the topic of demographic crisis. One-third of the way into the speech, he turns away from what he calls his "digression of a demographic order" [digressione d'ordine demografico],[37] and instead takes up an "exam of the bureaucratic organization of the nation" [esame dell'assetto amministrativo della nazione][38] that is composed of a lengthy and rather monotonous list of successful fascist initiatives, including the geographical reorganization of the provinces, the re-ordering of regional bureaucracy, the reform of police cadre, and fascist campaigns against organized crime. Neither does he return to the topic of demographic crisis in the final section of the speech, but instead moves to the topic of "general, current, and future political policy of the State" [direttive politiche, generali attuali e future dello Stato], which consists primarily of a description of the elimination of antifascist political opposition.[39] When read in light of an economy of crisis, this shift in the Ascension Day speech points not to the consummation of the fascist project – insofar as it is in essence a very long list of the regime's successes – but to a "more serious and formless threat," as Derrida puts it: the anxious repetition of successes suggests the fragility of the fascist project and the limitations of the fascist reproductive fantasy – even if Mussolini were to win the demographic battle by reaching his goal of sixty million Italians this anxious repetition points to the threat that he may nevertheless fail to transform the nation.

When one reads this speech carefully one notes that it is not simply the absence of physical bodies (more babies) that can bring about Italy's demise. The "destiny of nations" is not simply "linked to demographic power," as Mussolini asserts at the beginning of his speech but, as he insinuates in the latter sections, to something much more abstract and much more important: to the spirit of the Italian people. While Mussolini is certain of his ability to transform the bureaucratic structures of the nation and state, he is not as confident in his ability to instil the fascist spirit into the undisciplined and unruly Italian population. This uncertainty explains his excursus. He cannot yet say that fascism has transformed the Italian people and thus is compelled to dedicate a large portion of the speech to the ways in which fascism has definitively changed the nation and state. Notably, he imagines not only a transformation of Italy's physical "features" but "*most of all* her spirit."[40] In his eyes Italians are a people that are still "perfecting themselves, refining themselves, organizing themselves" [vanno perfezionandosi, raffinandosi, organizzandosi] – and they still have a lot of work to do.[41]

As is well known, Mussolini dreamed not only of "making Italians," as Massimo D'Azeglio once put it, but of completely remaking them through and within the bounds of the fascist state.[42] But whether the Italian individual would in fact see his or her relation to the state in such a seamless manner is a doubt that continually plagued him. As historian Emilio Gentile points out: "Mussolini had a rather poor opinion about the people he governed, in spite of his public elegies and attestations of esteem. In reality, he felt himself in a state of permanent war against the alleged 'Italian character.'"[43] Gentile reinforces this point with a quote from the diaries of the fervent ideologue Giuseppe Bottai, who candidly wrote in the late 1930s that Mussolini's "antagonist is this [Italian] people" [il suo antagonista è questo popolo].[44] The dictator, Bottai said, felt that Italians resisted "thinking and seeing 'big'" [a pensare e vedere 'grande'].[45] If Italians failed to fall in line with fascist doctrine, then the strong state and the fascistized nation that Mussolini envisions at the end of the Ascension Day speech could never be realized – no matter how great their number.

Indeed, the limitations of fascist power are present in Mussolini's admonition relatively early on in the speech that "laws are like medicine: they help when given to an organism that is still capable of reacting but when given to an organism that is close to death, they speed up the end due to their fatal congestions" [Le leggi sono come le medicine: date ad un organismo che è ancora capace di qualche reazione, giovano; date ad un organismo vicino alla decomposizione, ne affrettano, per le loro congestioni fatali, la fine].[46] Mussolini and his regime are doing all they can to save Italy by reforming the nation's infrastructure, including the legal infrastructure, but it is the Italian population that will evidently decide the nation's fate. Mussolini's concerns once again come to light when he speaks about the difference between public and moral order in the last section of the speech:

> Perfect public order can exist with profound moral disorder. We must occupy ourselves with moral order, not public order, because we have enough manpower for public order, in the policing sense of the word. We must instead occupy ourselves with moral order and, working intensely, we must aspire for the bond between the masses and the regime to be ever more vast, ever more steadfast, and ever more knowing.

> Ci può essere un ordine pubblico perfetto, e ci può essere un disordine morale profondo. Dobbiamo preoccuparci dell'ordine morale, non dell'ordine pubblico, perché per l'ordine pubblico, nel senso poliziesco della parola, abbiamo forze sufficienti; dobbiamo invece preoccuparci dell'ordine morale e dobbiamo volere, lavorando in profondo, che l'adesione tra le masse e il regime sia sempre più vasta, sempre più salda, sempre più consapevole.[47]

The economy of crisis operative in the Ascension Day speech, then, works to validate fascistization as a larger cultural enterprise on the one hand, and on the other to cover over the fact that what threatens the realization of a strong fascist nation comes from an internal rather than an external source. By mapping out the transformation of the nation that has already been carried out, as well as that which is yet to be inaugurated, Mussolini proclaims imminent victory over the demographic crisis at hand – a victory not just *for* but *of* the recently installed regime.

One can cull many examples from Mussolini's speeches and writings that illustrate a fascist economy of crisis put to differing political ends. For my purposes the most interesting of these writings are those that focus on demographic crisis. Let us take as another example the essay "Il numero come forza" ["Numbers as Power"], published on

1 September 1928, just over one year after the Ascension Day Speech.[48] It initially came out in the fascist journal *Gerarchia* and eventually was republished as a preface to the Italian edition of German statistician Richard Korherr's book *Regresso delle nascite*. As in the Ascension Day speech, Mussolini warns that the nation is at a crossroads, a crisis point, because of its low birth rate: "We are at a tragic phase of the phenomenon. Cradles are empty and cemeteries are growing" [Siamo alla fase tragica del fenomeno. Le culle sono vuote ed i cimiteri si allargano].[49] And, as in the Ascension Day speech, the spirit of the population is more essential to Italy's salvation than their number: "I believe that demographic legislation … can eliminate or in any case slow the phenomenon, if the social organism to which it is applied is still capable of reaction. In this case, morals and the religious consciousness of the individual are more important than formal laws" [io credo che le leggi demografiche … possono annullare o comunque ritardare il fenomeno, se l'organismo sociale al quale si applicano è ancora capace di reazione. In questo caso più che le leggi formali vale il costume morale e soprattutto la coscienza religiosa dell'individuo].[50] Indeed, this essay expresses many of the same ideological concerns as the Ascension Day speech – including concern about the fecundity or virility of the Italian race. But although Mussolini famously says in the Ascension Day speech, "We must … seriously watch over the destiny of the race, we must nurture the race" [Bisogna … vigilare seriamente sul destino della razza, bisogna curare la razza], racial anxiety remains in the background as an atmospheric albeit pervasive concern.[51] In "Il numero come forza," however, racial degeneration is explicitly featured as a key element in a connotative chain of associations linked to demographic crisis.

In this latter essay Mussolini speaks of the pathological rapid growth of urban centres, and ties it to the decline of the nation as well as to the decline of the white race:

> The city is dying, [and] the nation, without the vital lymph of the youth of new generations, can no longer fight … This happened. This can happen again. This will happen, and not only on the level of the city or nation but on an infinitely greater and more important level: the entire white race, the race of the West, can become submerged by the other races of colour that are multiplying at a rate unknown to ours.

> La città muore, la nazione – senza più le linfe vitali della giovinezza delle nuove generazioni – non può più resistere … Ciò è accaduto. Ciò può ancora accedere. Ciò accadrà e non soltanto fra città o nazioni, ma in un

> ordine di grandezze infinitamente maggiore: la intera razza bianca, la razza dell'Occidente, può venire sommersa dalle altre razze di colore che si moltiplicano con un ritmo ignoto alla nostra.[52]

The dictator describes an untimely death using the past declarative "this happened," which morphs through the possibility that "this can happen again" and once again morphs into the definitive future "this will happen." This rapid progression of verbs suggests an equally rapid extinction that spreads from the city, to the nation, to the "more important level" of the "entire white race." This speech illustrates what one might call "crisis creep," or the metonymic sliding between one crisis situation and another. In this case, the falling birth rate and racial degeneration are construed as mutually interdependent. And just as the contagion of sterility spreads from city to nation to the Western world, so do the inferior races of Asia and Africa multiply at an unimaginable rate. This fatal combination of events will purportedly lead to the extinction of the white race. Once this metonymic chain of equivalence is established, invoking one type of crisis automatically invokes the other. What is more, as the scale of demographic crisis is magnified, so are the consequences of inaction. Not having any or enough children could directly contribute to the fall not only of fascist Italy but also of Western Europe and of the white race as a whole – in essence, it could contribute to the fall of Western civilization.

Crisis creep is figured in this speech as a sustained crisis of boundaries with regard to race. First, Mussolini depicts the transgression of geographical boundaries of race when Africans and Asians no longer stay on their respective continents. To the question "Are Negroes and Chinamen at the door?" [Negri e gialli sono dunque alle porte?], Mussolini answers quite simply "Yes" [Sì].[53] What is particularly frightening, however, is not simply the fact that these races are increasing in number and knocking at Italy's door, but that this increase corresponds to an elevated consciousness, or what he might call spirit (exactly that which is lacking in Italians): "Yes, they are at the door, and not only as a result of their fecundity but also as a result of the consciousness that they have developed about their race and its future in the world" [Sì, sono alle porte e non soltanto per la loro fecondità ma anche per la coscienza che essi hanno preso della loro razza e del suo avvenire nel mondo].[54] Mussolini then gives a concrete, bodily form to the abstract idea of the transgression of racial boundaries. He speaks of the meteoric rise of the black population of the United States and paints a fearful image of how the "ultra fecund" black body can suddenly turn into "compact masses of negroes" rising up in violent and bloody revolt against the civilized forces of order:

> "In New York there is a large neighbourhood, Harlem, populated exclusively by negroes. A serious revolt by the negroes broke out last July, in the above-named neighborhood, and was suppressed with difficulty by the police after a night of bloody conflicts in which they found themselves facing compact masses of negroes"
>
> C'è un grande quartiere di New York, Harlem, popolato esclusivamente di negri. Una grave rivolta di negri scoppiata del luglio scorso in detto quartiere, fu a stento domata, dopo una notte di conflitti sanguinosi, dalla polizia, che si trovò di fronte masse compatte di negri.[55]

The representation of these "compact masses of negroes" reifies the threat of the political organization of the racial other as well as the threatening breakdown of an established racial hierarchy – threats that seem to have been just barely suppressed by the police. But the crisis is not over. This is just the beginning. Mussolini cautions his readers that "the warning bells are ringing" [Le campane d'allarme squillano].[56]

The figuration of a catastrophic rupture of boundaries and of a dangerous demographic crisis that is tightly bound to racial crisis is predictably attenuated in this speech by the comforting reinscription of racial hierarchy and corresponding social order: Mussolini insists that Italy's countryside is demographically healthy and that one of its most geographically liminal spaces, Sicily, is racially pure. In a passage shortly after the description of the revolt in Harlem, Mussolini makes certain "corrections" to Richard Korherr's book since, in his opinion, the German statistician's work reflects "certain inaccuracies as far as Italy is concerned" [alcune inesattezze per ciò che concerne l'Italia]:[57]

> If doctor Korherr takes a trip to Italy he will be convinced that:
>
> > a) it's not true that the countryside of Piedmont, Lombardy, Tuscany, Romagna, and Sicily are particularly in demographic decline, and
> > b) it's not true that the blacks have gotten as far as Sicily.
>
> Instead, the exact opposite is true. That is, it is true that Sicilians have planted themselves in numerous and compact masses in Roman Africa, while in Sicily there are only half a dozen people of colour made up of deportees who are Senussi and of Semitic origin.

Se il dott. Korherr farà un viaggio in Italia si convincerà:

a) che non è vero che le campagne del Piemonte, Lombardia, Toscana, Romagna, Sicilia siano in particolare decadenza demografica;
b) che non è vero che i negri si spingano sino in Sicilia.

È vero invece – nettamente – il contrario. È vero cioè che i siciliani si sono piantati in masse numerose e compatte nell'Africa romana, mentre in Sicilia di gente di colore non ci sono che messa dozzina di deportati senussiti e di origine semita.[58]

Turning the "compact masses" from black to Sicilian, Mussolini in effect domesticates the menacing threat of racial decline that rears its head, and puts it in its proper place within a fascist economy of crisis.

But if crisis creeps, then so does its cure. For example, as Mussolini argues in his "Speech to Physicians" ["Discorso ai medici"] (22 November 1931), not only economists but doctors can help to address the economic crisis:

People don't ask only if the bronchitis of a family member will go away sooner or later, but they sometimes ask if the economic crisis will pass sooner or later ... if the physician is a convinced fascist, not only a cardholder but one of the faithful, he will speak wisely and will say ... that the fascist Government has done, is doing, and will do everything possible to alleviate the consequences of this crisis for the Italian population.

La gente non domanda soltanto se la bronchite di un familiare passerà più o meno presto, ma domanda magari se la crisi economica passerà più o meno presto ... se il medico è fascista convinto, non solo per la tessera ma per la fede, dirà le parole della saggezza e dirà ... che il Governo fascista ha fatto, fa e farà il possibile perché le conseguenze di questa crisi siano alleviate per il popolo italiano.[59]

Fascist doctors, Mussolini implies, can and indeed must be responsible for addressing the population's physical maladies but also – and perhaps more importantly – their spiritual maladies. Any doubts about the system of fascist governance and any failure to believe in its ultimate victory over the crisis at hand can be cured by a "convinced fascist," no matter what their profession.

If we pull back for a moment to reflect on the larger picture, it is evident that when confronted with demographic crisis – whether expressed in terms of an obsession with quantity (population numbers) or with quality (racial degeneration) – what distinguishes Italian fascism from many other similar political movements is the central role occupied by the reproductive fantasy (with its emphasis on fertility, virility, and reproductive bodies) in the regime's response to crisis. As historian Maria S. Quine points out, Italian fascism's emphasis on these matters should not be underestimated; she delineates a "distinct Italian eugeni-fascism which was predicated on a notion of biological race and focused determinedly on a desire to preserve, protect, and enhance fertility."[60] Quine argues that Italian fascism "pursued a 'total' and totalizing biopolitical program no less obsessively than the Nazi regime did."[61] "But," she continues, "Fascist Italy's overriding racio-biological objective was different from that of Nazi Germany. Italian fascism sought to increase, by each and every socio-biological and repro-technological means, racial prolificity, rather than safeguard racial purity."[62] This emphasis on increasing rather than safeguarding led to the privileging of the positive rather than the more spectacular negative eugenic measures (sterilization, elimination), and may in part account for why the former have been largely overlooked or underestimated. Quine argues convincingly, however, that these measures are no less important and deserve to be considered for their own merit rather than measured against those of the Nazi regime. Given the central role of the reproductive fantasy in the regime's ideological program, the *donna-crisi* serves as a revealing flashpoint for the conflict between the desires of individuals (whether they be about reproductive choices or the latest fashions to follow) and the political and ideological goals of the regime.

Although Mussolini does not mention the crisis-woman by name in the writings I cite above, we know that we are not far from her territory since – as I point out in chapter 2 – fascist discourse linked the *donna-crisi* to falling birthrates, social disease, racial degeneration, and unchecked urban expansion. Indeed, the crisis-woman lurks just out of sight in Mussolini's 1931 "Speech to the Doctors" when he condemns "the fashion of excessive weight loss" [la moda del dimagramento eccessivo] as one of the major "deformations of contemporary civilization" [storture della civiltà contemporanea].[63] Articulating a similar preoccupation with racial integrity as in "Il numero come forza," Mussolini asserts that this modern fashion fad "weakens the race and also has repercussions of an economic nature" [indebolisce la razza ed ha delle ripercussioni anche d'ordine e di natura economica] (60). Moreover, we see a similar preoccupation with the fascistization of the

Italian spirit as in the Ascension Day speech when he goes on to say that "prejudices of fashion" [pregiudizi della moda] such as that of excessive weight loss are "inevitable weaknesses of the human spirit" [debolezze inevitabili dello spirito umano].[64]

Once the figure of the crisis-woman is actually introduced onto the Italian social, political, and cultural scene in 1931, she has a specific structural and performative role in a fascist economy of crisis. With regard to the former she signifies pure difference, and with regard to the latter she facilitates the seamless operation of an economy of crisis by embodying a purported threat and thus making it conquerable. Camilla Nervi's article "Donna 'crisi,'" discussed in chapter 2, illustrates this mechanism quite clearly. For Nervi, as we will recall, deviance and disease is manifest above all in the crisis-woman's body. Nervi reifies the deadening homogeneity of modernity in the crisis-woman's body insofar as every *donna-crisi* is "equally slender and stylized" [egualmente sottili e stilizzate]; she reifies the dangerous blurring of gender lines in the crisis-woman's body insofar as it comes "a bit too close to the masculine body type" [un po' troppo al tipo morfologico mascolino]; the "caved-in cheeks" [guance smunte], "anemic eyes" [occhi anemici], and "false floridness" [finta floridezza] of the crisis-woman make concrete her connection to the nineteenth-century pathology of consumption and thus to bourgeois decadence; finally, the body of the crisis woman demonstrates her inability carry out the maternal function since her "internal organs" [organi interni] have been damaged by using fashionable modern apparatuses such as "elastic girdles" [fasce elastiche].[65] A series of threats to the integrity of the larger social body are embodied in the crisis-woman, and Nervi resolutely calls for her elimination. In fact, she even performatively enacts that elimination when she says that the physique of the crisis-woman "is about to disappear" [sta per scomparire].[66] Following in the footsteps of Mussolini, however, Nervi seems to be ultimately preoccupied not so much with the conquerable body of the crisis woman as the potentially unruly spirit of the modern Italian woman: "more than the physical aspects, it is the spiritual direction of woman that society can and must focus on" [più che il fisico, è l'indirizzo spirituale della donna che può e deve richiamare l'attenzione della società].[67] Nervi, like Mussolini, reminds her reader that although the crisis-woman "is about to disappear," relentless discipline and regulation is nevertheless required on the part of individual Italian women to ensure that they are not touched by the critical malady that infects so many of their peers.

In sum, the rhetorical and ideological effects of the term "crisis" are indeed far reaching within fascist discourse. The exhaustive assertion of the primacy of crisis at all levels of culture was not simply a reflection of the tumultuous historical period out of which fascism was born, but a tactical strategy that served specific political and ideological goals. Looking at this broader economy of crisis helps us to see the crisis-woman as part of a larger network of signification that has both semantic *and* pragmatic effects and that works to establish fascism as an uncontestable force, yet a force that upon closer examination must anxiously reassert itself over and over again

Conclusion

The Decline of the Donna-crisi

By the mid 1930s, as the economic crisis began to abate so too did verbal and pictorial attacks on the crisis-woman, eventually dying out. In the end, the regime's campaign against the dreaded, deadly *donna-crisi* lasted only three short years: from 1931 to 1934. Crisis as a fascist mode of political discourse, however, continued. Its racial inflections and preoccupation with the health of the national body were buoyed by events such as the invasion of Ethiopia and the impending world war – a rich topic for further study.

Although the life of the crisis-woman may have been brief, her memory has been enduring. Despite the fact that until now only a handful of primary sources have documented her existence, the *donna-crisi* is mentioned in nearly every comprehensive scholarly study of women under the fascist regime and has been generally taken as a widespread phenomenon of the period. Even Umberto Eco, one of Italy's most well-known polymaths, in his 2004 novel *The Mysterious Flame of Queen Loana* speaks of the abject "'crisis woman' of our own plutocratic past" who stood in opposition to the regime's idealized "splendid baby-making machines" with their "large breasts and soft curves."[1] Perhaps the *donna-crisi* endures in scholarly and the broader cultural memory in part because she has been understood in the oppositional paradigm that Eco proposes: *donna-crisi* versus *donna-madre*, sterile versus fecund, ill versus healthy, urbane versus rural, useless versus productive, negative versus positive. As I have shown throughout this book, however, such a paradigm can neither account for the complexities of the discursive inscription of power upon the female body nor for the particular role of the female body in fascist thought. As we have seen, the *donna-crisi* was a crucial product of fascist ideology because she served as a necessary "other" against which idealized images of fascist female subjectivity were built and measured: Mussolini's "sposa e madre esemplare," or "ideal wife and mother," was such a powerful symbol in part because abject figures like the crisis-woman stood as her opposite. We have also observed the ways in which Italian fascism placed special emphasis on the control and disciplinary surveillance of the female body because of its potential fertility, and how the regime incited women – all women: so-called crisis-women, mothers, young women, and others – to relentlessly patrol their bodies for possible signs of deviance. In the end, the crisis-woman never managed to supplant Italy's heterogeneous modern woman, as the regime so desired, but coexisted side by side with her as well as hegemonic positive models of femininity like the *donna-madre* and the *donna-nuova*. The power of these figures was not destabilized precisely because all of them supported and were an integral part of a fascist politics of the body in both productive and repressive ways. By studying the inflections and articulation of the *donna-crisi* in fascist culture, we not only have gained a fuller understanding of the spectrum of representations of femininity that existed under the regime but, more importantly, have begun to understand the multifaceted operations of power through which they operated, a project that is crucial to gaining a clearer picture of this formative period in the social, cultural, and political history of the Italian nation.

Appendixes

A. Lyrics to "Mah, cos'è questa crisi?" (1933)
by Rodolfo De Angelis

Si lamenta l'impresario che il teatro più non va,
The director laments that the theatre is no longer popular,

ma non sa rendere vario lo spettacolo che dà… ah, la crisi!!
But he doesn't know how to vary the type of show he gives … oh, the crisis!!

Mah cos'è questa crisi? Mah cos'è questa crisi?
So, what is this crisis? So, what is this crisis?

metta in scena un buon autore, faccia agire un grande attore
Put a good author on stage, let a great actor act

e vedrà che la crisi passerà!
And you'll see that the crisis will pass.

Un riccone avaro e vecchio dice, ahimè, così non va,
A stingy old man says, oh dear, things are not well

vedo nero nello specchio, chissà come finirà … ah, la crisi!!
The future looks bad, who knows what will happen … oh, the crisis!!

Mah cos'è questa crisi? Mah cos'è questa crisi?
So, what is this crisis? So, what is this crisis?

Cavi fuori i portafogli, metta in giro i grossi fogli, e vedrà che la crisi finirà!
Pull out your wallets, lay down the big bucks, and you'll see that the crisis will pass!

Si lamenta Nicodemo della crisi, lui che va
The high roller complains of the crisis, he who goes

nel Casino di San Remo, a giocare al baccarà ... ah, la crisi!!
to the casino at San Remo, to play blackjack ... oh, the crisis!!

Mah cos'è questa crisi? Mah cos'è questa crisi?
So, what is this crisis? So, what is this crisis?

Lasci stare il gavazzare, cerchi un po' di lavorare e vedrà che la crisi passerà!
Stop fooling around, try to work a bit and you'll see that the crisis will pass!

Tutte quante le nazioni si lamentano così,
All of the nations have the same lament

conferenze, riunioni, ma si resta sempre lì ... ah, la crisi!!
Conferences, meetings, but things never change ... oh, the crisis!!

Mah cos'è questa crisi? Mah cos'è questa crisi?
So, what is this crisis? So, what is this crisis?

Rinunziate all'opinione della parte del leone e chissà che la crisi finirà!
Let go of the majority opinion and, who knows, the crisis might just pass!

L'esercente poveretto non sa più che cosa far
The poor shop-owner no longer knows what to do,

e contempla quel cassetto che riempiva di danar... ah, la crisi!!
and contemplates that drawer which he once filled with money ... oh, the crisis!!

Mah cos'è questa crisi? Mah cos'è questa crisi?
So, what is this crisis? So, what is this crisis?

Si contenti guadagnare quel che è giusto e non grattare e vedrà che la crisi passerà!
Rather than stealing, content yourself with earning what's fair and you'll see that the crisis will pass!

E persin' la donna bella ha alla crisi s'intonò,
And even the beautiful woman joins in the crisis

e per far la linea snella digiunando, sospirò.... ah la crisi!!
To achieve a slim figure she fasts and sighs ... oh, the crisis!!

Mah cos'è questa crisi? Mah cos'è questa crisi?
So, what is this crisis? So, what is this crisis?

Mangi un sacco di patate, non mi sprechi le nottate e vedrà che la curva tornerà!
Eat a bunch of potatoes, don't waste my nights, and you'll see that the curves will return!

Mah cos'è questa crisi? Mah cos'è questa crisi?
So, what is this crisis? So, what is this crisis?

Chi ce li ha, li metta fuori, circolare miei signori e chissà che la crisi finirà!
Those who've got it, pull it out! Go out a bit my friends and, who knows, the crisis might just pass away!

B. Lyrics to "Donna crisi" (1933) by Romolo Balzani

Da quanno te sei messa a fà la cura d'Olivù
Since you've started your Hollywood diet-regime,

Ninetta mia adorata nun t'ariconosco più!
My sweet Ninetta, I can't recognize you!

A me parevi invece tanto bella
You seemed so beautiful to me,

quann'eri un pochettino grassottella!
when you were a bit chubby!

E quanno uscimo insieme co' la vita che ciài tu
And when we go out, with the waist that you've got now,

me pare che me porto er bastoncino de bambù!
I feel like I'm carrying around a stick of bamboo!

Co' te che posso facce a esse sincera?
To be honest, what can I do with you?

t'adoperò pe' asta de bandiera!
I'll use you as a staff for a flag!

Tu pe' pranzo e colazione so che magni, Nina mia,
My Nina, I know what you eat for breakfast and lunch,

una coccia de limone co' tre mele alla giudìa,
a slice of lemon with three apples alla giudìa

un ciccetto d'insalata, un pezzetto de grisino,
a sprig of salad, and a piece of a breadstick,

n'alicetta marinata, senza frutta e senza vino …
a marinated anchovy, without fruit and without wine …

e poi, come rimedio che nun falla,
and then, as a remedy that never fails,

te bevi un bicchieruccio d'acqua calla!
you drink a glass of hot water!

Siccome tu me piaci e io un conzijo te vojo dà,
Since I like you, I want to give you some advice,

Ninetta mia adorata ... su, arimmettete a magnà!
my sweet Ninetta ... come on, start eating again!

Nun te conviè de esse 'no stoppino,
It's not good for you to be a candlewick,

ritorna la bistecca ar filoncino!
go back to being a steak filet!

La donna crisi ormai tu lo sai che nun va più
You know by now that the crisis-woman is not in style anymore,

perciò nun ostinatte a fa la cura d'Olivù!
so don't persist in your Hollywood cure!

Io te vorrebbe vede bianca e rossa:
I'd like to see your cheeks red and white:

ahò! me so stufato a rosicamme l'ossa!
ohi! I'm sick of chewing on a bone!

Vai ar mècce der pallone, a le corse de li cani
You go to soccer games, to dog races,

fai lo sport a perfezione, sòni er piano a quattro mani ...
you practice sports perfectly, you play the piano for four hands ...

ma però pe' fà l'amore nun ciài mai un minuto spiccio!
but you never have a spare minute for lovemaking!

Si te sposo dice er core: "Nina mia, sta qui l'impiccio!":
My heart says that if I marry you: "My Nina, here is the problem!"

perché p'avé li fiji e esse felice ... me toccherà comprà l'incubatrice!
In order to have children and be happy ... I'll have to buy an incubator!

E si seguiti a cibatte de grisini e de limone
And if you keep on eating breadsticks and lemons,

io nun posso più sposatte, mica vojo fa er frescone!
I won't be able to marry you, I certainly don't want to come off as a dim-wit!

E nun vojo che la gente dica: "Quello s'è scemito!"
And I don't want people to say: "He's turned stupid!"

Co' la donna trasparente nun conviè da fa er marito!
It doesn't pay to marry a transparent woman!

Perché la donna crisi nun è bella,
Because the crisis-woman isn't pretty,

ce vò 'na donna fatta a pagnottella!
One needs a woman made like a sandwich!

C. Captions for "Donna crisi utilitaria" by Mameli Barbara, published in *Marc'Aurelio* (1933)

Grida allegro il sor Pasquale;
Mr Pasquale happily cries

–Oggi è festa nazionale!
"Today is a national holiday!"

E si affretta con ardore
And with ardour he rushes

ad esporre il tricolore.
to put the tricolour on display.

Da un casson, con aria fiera,
From a trunk, with a proud air

tira fuori la bandiera,
he pulls out the flag,

ammirandola, entusiasta …
admiring it enthusiastically …

Ma che fare? Manca l'asta!
But what to do? There is no staff!

Sor Pasquale non resta in ozio,
He rushes to the store,

si precipita al negozio,
Mr Pasquale does not delay,

ma oggi è festa, e come d'uso,
but finds that it is closed.

il negozio trova chiuso.
as is custom on a holiday.

Torna a casa disperato,
Returning home, despairing and

e s'abbatte, scoraggiato;
discouraged, he loses heart;

Donna Crisi, in quel frangente,
Crisis Woman, at that moment

sta a guardare e non fa niente.
  looks on and does nothing.

Sor Pasquale balza in aria:
  Mr Pasquale jumps into the air

"Un'idea straordinaria!
  "An extraordinary idea!

Ecco alfin trovata l'asta:
  Here at last the staff is found:

C'è mia moglie: è quanto basta!"
  There's my wife: all that's needed!"

Ora espone il Sor Pasquale
  Now Mr Pasquale displays

la bandiera nazionale:
  the flag of our nation:

Donna Crisi, all'occasione,
  Crisis Woman can serve as a pole

può servire da bastone.
  for this occasion.

D. Captions for "Donna crisi inutilitaria" by Mameli Barbara, published in *Marc'Aurelio* (1933)

La Regina Cusaranca
  Queen Cusaranca

ha riunito i suoi guerrieri:
  has gathered her warriors:

vuol gustar la carne bianca
she wants to taste white meat

n'è digiuna davant'ieri.
she hasn't had any since the day before yesterday.

I cannibali nascosti
The hidden cannibals

fiutan già la carovana
spy the caravan

voglion proprio a tutti i costi
at all costs, they want

soddisfare la sovrana.
to satisfy the queen.

Su una palma lì vicina
Up a nearby palm tree

è salito adesso un negro:
a black man has now climbed:

"Quanta buona selvaggina,"
"How much good game,"

egli annuncia tutto allegro.
he happily announces.

E con urli prolungati
With long cries

pregustando la cuccagna
almost tasting the abundance

dan l'assalto ai disgraziati
they assail this poor group

che han levato le calcagna.
who have began to run.

Ma la caccia è sfortunata
But the hunt is not successful

e il bottino assai scadente
and the loot is rather scarce

fra i cannibali è restata
among the cannibals has remained

donna crisi solamente.
only the crisis-woman.

La sovrana assai indignata
The queen, rather indignant,

ora grida a più non posso:
now shouts, I can no more:

"La quaresima è passata.
"The Lenten fast is over.

Cosa spolpo, da quest'osso?"
What can I get off this bone?"

Notes

Introduction

1 Throughout this book, unless otherwise noted, all translations of primary source material are mine.

2 The *donna-crisi* is linked here to nineteenth-century figures that disrupt established conventions of gendered identity. See, for example, Karl Heinrich Ulrichs's writings on the third sex in *The Riddle of "Man-Manly" Love*, or Marjorie Garber's *Vested Interests* for contemporary criticism.

3 De Grazia, *How Fascism Ruled Women*, 73.

4 See also de Grazia's essay "Nationalizing Women."

5 In addition, see Cannistraro's foundational study *La fabbrica del consenso* (89 as well as Appendix 3, "Direttive per la stampa di Polverelli"), and Rossana Bossaglia's "The Iconography of the Italian Novecento."

6 Horn, *Social Bodies*, 12.

7 See Foucault's *Discipline and Punish*.

8 Butler's idea that it is precisely "through the force of exclusion and abjection" that "the subject is constituted" underlies my reading of the figure of the *donna-crisi* in relation to positive models of fascist subjectivity (*Bodies That Matter*, 3). Moreover, her argument that "certain abject zones within sociality" (242) threaten to dissolve the subject is crucial to my analysis of just how the crisis-woman operates as a figure of fascist propaganda.

9 Derrida, "Economies de la crise," 4.

10 See Offen, *European Feminisms*, and de Grazia, *How Fascism Ruled Women* (especially chap. 2).

11 Steele, *Fashion and Eroticism*, 230. On the emergence of this new physical type see also Aspesi, *Il Lusso e l'autarchia;* Buttazzi, *1922–1943: Vent'anni di moda italiana;* Guenther, *Nazi Chic?;* Laver, *Women's Dress*; and Roberts,

Civilization without Sexes, "Gender, Consumption, and Commodity Culture," and "Samson and Delilah Revisited."

12 Butazzi, *1922–1943: Vent'anni di moda italiana,* 13.

13 Although the newly established fascist regime increasingly attempted to control all forms of cultural production – for example through expanding limitations on the press – by no means was there complete or seamless censorship or review of images of women, especially in the realm of popular cultural production directed at a female audience.

14 Gronberg makes this point when she says: "As numerous scholars have argued, the 1920s modern woman – both the German *neue Frau* and the French *femme moderne* – was a social stereotype, the product of economic and political change after the First World War. Maud Lavin points to the multiple uses of the term *new woman* and claims that it is best considered as 'a cumulative perception of female stereotypes.' Lynne Frame cites three examples: Gretchen, girl, and *garçonne*. Similarly in her work on France, Mary Louise Roberts has highlighted different images of women at this period of *la femme moderne – la mère* and *la femme seule*. She considers the figure of the *femme moderne* as a kind of symbol, a means by which postwar French society attempted to come to terms with loss and cultural change" ("Sonia Delaunay's Simultaneous Fashions and the Modern Woman," 111). See also Chadwick and Latimer, *The Modern Woman Revisited*, and Dowling, "The Decadent and the New Woman."

15 Chadwick and Latimer, *The Modern Woman Revisited*, 3.

16 Aspesi, *Il Lusso e l'autarchia,* 43.

17 Ibid., 43. Philip Cannistraro makes the same observation in the appendix to *La fabbrica del consenso*, 421–2.

18 Mary Louise Roberts shows in *Civilization without Sexes* that a similar backlash against the figure of the modern woman took place in France at this time. In addition, writing specifically about the French context, Giulia Veronesi identifies a female type that is much like the crisis-woman. She shows a thin, modern woman identified, in the words of Jeanne Lanvin, as the "'flat' woman, later known as the 'Depression woman'" (*Into the Twenties*, unnumbered page, image 168). In her appendix, she ties this thin, modern figure to that of the flapper: "The flapper was the feminine type of the twenties; later she was to return, more or less, as *la femme de trente ans.* This new type was called the 'depression woman'" (348). The important difference between the Italian and French contexts is the way in which the figure of the crisis-woman was used by the regime to support its projects and ideals.

19 For census figures see the Istituto Nazionale di Statistica (ISTAT) website (http://www.istat.it/it/). Most scholars agree with Massimo Livi-Bacci, a

well-respected historian of Italian fertility, who argues that "on the whole, the direct long-range effects of the fascist demographic policy seem to have been very modest, if any existed at all" (*A History of Italian Fertility*, 280).

20 For more information on the repressive measures of demographic policy see de Grazia, *How Fascism Ruled Women*, chap. 3, and Ipsen, *Dictating Demography*.

21 Mussolini, *Opera Omnia*, vol. 22, 367.

22 In addition to Bynum's *Holy Feast and Holy Fast*, see also Rudolph Bell's *Holy Anorexia*.

23 See chap. 4 of Gianni Toniolo's *L'economia dell'Italia fascista* for an extended description of unemployment in this period.

24 See Appendix A for full lyrics in the original Italian and in translation.

25 Guardi, "La crisi dell'amore," 13. *Excelsior* was a monthly, and later weekly, magazine that focused on the entertainment industry and the world fine arts and was published in Milan.

26 Advertisement for Jodont toothpaste entitled "Ah, la crisi!" *Il Travaso delle idee* 33, no. 13 (March 1933): 2.

27 Vera, "Previsioni," 24.

28 For more on the fashions of the Depression Era, see Aspesi, *Il Lusso e l'autarchia*, 33–5.

Chapter 1

1 Steele, *Fashion and Eroticism*, 225.

2 Ibid., 227.

3 Brin, *Usi e costumi*, 80.

4 The excerpt is from Grillenzoni's article "I caratteri del fisico e del vestire considerati come fattori demografici" ["Characteristics of Physique and Dress Considered as Demographic Factors"]. Meldini reproduces this article in his book *Sposa e madre esemplare*, and gives it the amusing title "È brutta e sciamannata: Sarà di sicuro proficuo" [She's Ugly and Disheveled, She's Sure to be Prolific].

5 Mondello, *La nuova italiana*, 9.

6 Mag (pseud.), "Primi tepori estivi, primi abiti leggeri," 33.

7 For more on the editorial history of *Lidel* see Paulicelli, *Fashion under Fascism*; Buttazzi, *1922–1943: Vent'anni di moda italiana*; and De Longis, "Stampa femminile," 683. Both Buttazzi and Paulicelli stress the complex ideological roots of the magazine. Paulicelli underscores the combination of nationalism with a modern aesthetic. Buttazzi points out that De Liguoro, "who launched the magazine in 1919 … belonged to a circle of women who arrived at fascism, its earliest stages, through a nationalist

matrix with all its limitations – such as the sense of a 'mutilated victory' [in WWI], of a 'great nation which is the cradle of art,' and so on – but also participated in the type of 'Jacobin' aggression which marked the early fascists as an extremely heterogeneous group, even from a political point of view" (14).

8 Mag, "Primi tepori estivi, primi abiti leggeri," 33.

9 See Douglas's book *Purity and Danger.*

10 See, for example, Carolyn Walker Bynum's *Holy Feast and Holy Fast*. In the case of this narrative, however, rather than the female body exuding miraculous fluid, it is capable of erasure of a staining fluid.

11 Quoted in Wilson, *Adorned in Dreams*, 2.

12 Mag, "Primi tepori estivi, primi abiti leggeri," 33.

13 See Aspesi, *Il Lusso e l'autarchia;* Buttazzi, *1922–1943: Vent'anni di moda italiana;* and Mondello, *La nuova italiana*. Paulicelli, *Fashion under Fascism,* is one of the few scholars to analyse this magazine through close reading.

14 Mag, "Primi tepori estivi, primi abiti leggeri," 35–6.

15 The content of this second vignette cannot help but call to mind the psychoanalytic concept of masquerade, first theorized by Joan Riviere in 1929.

16 Mag, "Primi tepori estivi, primi abiti leggeri," 36.

17 Ibid., 36.

18 The association between long, loose hair and uncontrolled, threatening female sexuality is a common nineteenth-century literary trope. See, for example, Del Principe's *Rebellion, Death, and Aesthetics* – especially his chapter on Tarchetti's *Fosca.*

19 Although, as I suggest above, there is a parallel between the first vignette and hagiographic narratives of female saints that emphasized the miraculous transformation of (and in many ways the power of) the female body, this last vignette differs greatly from the first. The potential transformation (from long hair to short) is curtailed and entirely controlled by the male figure, and the emphasis is squarely on the misguided desire of the woman.

20 See, for example, de Grazia's "Nationalizing Women" and *How Fascism Ruled Women.* Also extremely relevant to this discussion is Angela McRobbie's "Bridging the Gap: Feminism, Fashion and Consumption," which argues that more attention must be paid to the fact that economically disadvantaged women were not able to engage in consumption practices in the same way as more privileged women and that, furthermore, they were often exploited by the fashion industry as producers of clothing and textiles.

21 For more on the destabilization implied by consumer culture in the fascist period, see Jacquline Reich's essay "Consuming Ideologies," about Mario

Camerini's film *Grandi magazzini,* whose narrative unfolds against the backdrop of the department store of the same name.

22 This appeal for moderation is quite common, and not only in Italy. See Roberts, *Civilization,* 81–2. Steele points out in *Fashion and Eroticism* that moderation was emphasized even in the less-restricted world of French fashion, 229–30.

23 See Tranfaglia's *La stampa del regime.*

24 Ibid., 168.

25 Ibid., 168.

26 Ibid., 168–9.

27 Ibid., 170.

28 Readers should recall that the term "modern woman" is used herein to refer to the non-fascist, cosmopolitan notion of the modern woman, whereas the terms *donna nuova* and *nuova italiana* are used to refer to the fascist representation of the modern woman in the vein of the *uomo nuovo,* as part of the larger fascist project of creating a new Italy.

29 De Grazia, *How Fascism Ruled Women,* 2; emphasis added. See that work for more specific examples that illustrate the manner in which the fascist state outwardly stated that it was modernizing women's roles in society while simultaneously restricting women to the domestic space and to traditional roles or, conversely, ways in which the fascist state said that it valued a return to tradition yet inadvertently emancipated women in ways it could not predict.

30 Ibid., 2. De Grazia goes on to argue that "mobilizing politics, modernizing social services, finally, the belligerent militarism of the 1930s, all had the unintended effect of undercutting conservative notions of female roles and family styles. In the process [of modernization], fascist institutions ordained new kinds of social involvement and recast older notions of maternity and fatherhood, femaleness and masculinity. As in other areas of society, the dictatorship claimed to be restoring the old, when, in spite of itself, it established much that was new" (2).

31 G.M., "Bellezza femminile italica," 7.

32 Vera, "La moda: Commenti e consigli," 22.

33 This gesture of classifying the body into empirical types is typical of positivism, a formative school of thought with regard to the crisis-woman; I discuss this influence more fully in chap. 2.

34 De Grazia, *How Fascism Ruled Women,* 14

35 Ronchi, "La moda italiana," 4.

36 Ibid., 4.

37 Ibid., 4.

38 Ibid., 4.
39 Piccoli, "Le grasse e le magre," 4.
40 Ibid., 4.
41 Ibid., 4.
42 Ibid., 5.
43 Butler, *Gender Trouble*, 134–5.

Chapter 2

1 Brin, *Usi e costumi*, 14–15.
2 Ibid., 14.
3 Gilman, *Picturing Health*, 51.
4 Ibid., 51.
5 Ibid., 51; emphasis added.
6 Although Pende is one of the most well-known signatories of this document, he was not involved in drafting it. In fact, the contents of the document opposed many of Pende's own theories of race. As a result he distanced himself from the document in several ways. For details, see chap. 3 of Gillette's *Racial Theories in Fascist Italy*.
7 As Carl Ipsen explains, constitutional science was a study "founded in particular on anthropometry, of the relationship between different body types ('brevilineal,' 'longilineal,' and intermedial types) and on the interconnections between various other characteristics of the human being: intellectual capacity, elements of personality, and eventual pathology" ("Pende," 358). Pende refers to his particular brand of constitutionalism as "orthogenesis," and his scientific method and theory link him to the positivist tradition.
8 Gibson makes the connection between Pende and Lombroso explicit in her article "Cesare Lombroso and Italian Criminology." There is much research still to be done on Lombroso's influence on science during the fascist period – a topic that is beyond the scope of my work here.
9 For more on this topic see Pick, *Faces of Degeneration*.
10 Ipsen, *Dictating Demography*, 186.
11 For an example of the *libretto* see Pende's *Trattato di biotipologia umana*.
12 Ipsen, "Pende," 358.
13 Pende, "Costituzione e fecondità," 80. As is the case with many scientific studies in this period, Pende's numerical data are not particularly convincing. The differences he finds are so close as to be indistinguishable to the naked eye; one wonders, then, about the larger cultural value he ascribes to these "types." The "maternal" biotype has hips that are 1.2 centimetres (not quite 0.5 inches) wider than the "normal" woman and shoulders that

are 0.4 centimeters (nearly 0.2 inches) narrower. Moreover, he ignores information that might contradict his claim. For example, he never considers the fact that women who have had children might have a larger distance between their hips *precisely because* they have had children and not because they are constitutionally predisposed to having more children.

14 Pende, "Costituzione e fecondità," 79; emphasis in original. It is interesting that both here and elsewhere Pende draws attention to the participation in this study of these *female* students or assistants, almost as if to legitimate his findings among women themselves. (See his mention of this same study in *Bonifica umana*.)

15 Ibid., 79; emphasis added.

16 Ibid., 79.

17 On the broader reach of positivist science in Italian culture during these years see, for example, Ben Ghiat's *Fascist Modernities*.

18 The term "*bonifica*" refers to land reclamation, but in the fascist context "*bonifica umana*" (literally, human reclamation) was the eugenicist project of improving the health of the Italian race. As many readers will know, rationalism was originally an architectural term but in the fascist context eventually came to broadly signify a modern, scientific method of working based on empirical research. Finally, as Pende explains himself, "*Political biology* is the science, founded simultaneously on scientific and empirical research, of man considered as a cell in the great social organism; it must, in a realistic and naturalistic age such as ours, guide men in government" [*Biologia politica* è la scienza che, fondata sullo studio scientifico ed empirico al tempo stesso, degli uomini, considerati come cellule del grande organismo sociale, e deve, in un'epoca realistica e naturalistica come la nostra, guidare gli uomini del governo] (*Bonifica umana*, 7). For an excellent discussion of organismic metaphors, such as the one employed in this passage, see Horn's *Social Bodies*.

19 Pende, *Bonifica umana*, 5.

20 The project of *bonifica integrale* – of which *bonifica umana* was a part – should be directly linked to the demographic initiative. As Luisa Passerini points out, "Demographic policy was not designed merely to increase the population but to carry out a clean-up operation … It is no accident that one of its manifestos was the Ascension Day speech of 1927 which insisted on the need to 'cleanse' the race, fusing together biological eugenicist concerns with the aims of a political purge" (*Fascism in Popular Memory*, 152).

21 Ipsen states that "Fascists and non-Fascists alike considered the demographic problem to be among the most pressing affecting Italian society; the "problem of problems" it would be called" (*Dictating Demography*, 2).

22 Pende, *Bonifica umana*, 191.

23 Ibid., 202. De Grazia gives the following illuminating statistics on women's work, which show just how important the female labour force was to the Italian economy despite the regime's concerns about working women: "In the 1930's, over one quarter of Italy's workforce was female, and one woman out of every four between the ages of 14 and 65 was economically active. In at least one and a half million Italian household – 16 percent of all in 1931 – women were the main breadwinners. In several million others they supplemented the family income" (*How Fascism Ruled Women*, 166). In short, for many families, women's work was a necessity rather than a choice.
24 Pende, *Bonifica umana*, 202.
25 Ibid., 204.
26 Ibid., 205.
27 Ibid., 206.
28 Rose, "Medicine, History and the Present," 55.
29 Ibid., 54.
30 Ibid., 54.
31 Pende, *Bonifica umana*, 210.
32 Ibid., 210; emphasis in original.
33 Ibid., 210.
34 Ibid., 210.
35 Ibid., 210.
36 Ibid., 211.
37 Ibid., 211.
38 Ibid., 212.
39 Ibid., 109.
40 Ibid., 209–10; emphasis added.
41 Ibid., 210.
42 See Kraus's "Forward vs. Reverse Gear" and Passerini's *Fascism in Popular Memory*. Kraus makes this politicized argument more forcefully than Passerini, but both present a variety of evidence to suggest that, particularly with regard to birth control and abortion, women were taking control of their bodies in ways that directly opposed the legislative mandates of the regime.
43 Fiducia, "Aberrazioni moderne," 59. The expression "thin as toothpicks" clearly recalls the type of wordplay typical of representations of the crisis-woman in satirical publications, which I shall discuss at length in the following chapter.
44 Ibid., 58–9.
45 Ibid., 59.
46 Ibid., 59.

47 Nervi was an occasional contributor to *Maternità ed Infanzia*, and is identified in other issues as a doctor. See, for example, the table of contents for the September 1927 issue.
48 Nervi, "Donna 'Crisi,'" 12.
49 Ibid., 12.
50 Ibid., 12.
51 Although my discussion focuses on the late nineteenth century, and on the writing of Cesare Lombroso in particular, I do not mean to suggest that this way of looking at the body does not have a long history. One might point, for example, to the fields of phrenology or physiognomy, which, of course, markedly influenced Lombroso's work.
52 For more on these devices and practices see Horn's *The Criminal Body*.
53 Here one is reminded of the negligible difference in hip and shoulder measurements of the maternal and non-maternal type in Pende's writing, discussed above.
54 Horn, *The Criminal Body*, 13.
55 Osborne, "On Anti-Medicine and Clinical Reason," 32.
56 Foucault, *The Birth of the Clinic*, xiii.
57 Moreover, this gaze is itself a "loquacious gaze" insofar as it is linked to the emergence of modern medicalized discourse (*The Birth of the Clinic*, xi). As Osborne describes, the clinical gaze is linked to "the production of a clinical description involving a presentation of symptoms and other factors relevant to the patient's history (swellings, effusions, breathing, colour of tongue, daily occupation and habits, nature of appetite, quantity of urine, nature of stools, relevant moral factors, etc.) and an account of findings at autopsy" ("On Anti-Medicine and Clinical Reason," 32).
58 Armstrong, *Political Anatomy of the Body*, 2.
59 Ibid., 2.
60 Horn, *The Criminal Body*, 52.
61 Ibid., 140; emphasis added.
62 Ibid, 141.
63 Ibid, 141.
64 Nervi, "Donna 'Crisi,'" 12.
65 Ibid., 12.
66 Ibid., 13
67 Pende, "Maternità, estetica," 8.
68 Ibid., 8.
69 Ibid., 8.
70 Ibid., 8.
71 Ibid., 8.

72 Spackman, *Fascist Virilities*, 131. Although Spackman's use of the term "re-semanticization" is more specific than mine in that, as she says, it "largely concerns the erasure of redeployment of socialist terminology" (131), I suggest that the term can equally apply within other discursive fields, such as the medical, which are crucial grounds for the politicized shaping of individual and social bodies.
73 Lawlor, *Consumption and Literature*, 46. See also Ott's *Fevered Lives*, Barnes's *The Making of a Social Disease*, and Gilman's *Franz Kafka, The Jewish Patient*.
74 Ibid., 43; emphasis added.
75 See Bynum's *Holy Feast and Holy Fast* and Bell's *Holy Anorexia*.
76 Bynum, *Holy Feast and Holy Fast*, 199.
77 Ibid., 200.
78 Brin, *Usi e costumi*, 14.
79 Ibid., 115–16.
80 See for example Gilman's *The Jew's Body* and Zizek's discussion of the Jew and anti-Semitism in *The Sublime Object* (esp. pp. 48–9 and 124–8).
81 Pick, *Faces of Degeneration*, 7. For more on degeneration theory see also chap. 4, "Heredity of Milieu," of Robert Nye's *Crime, Madness, and Politics* as well as Chamberlin and Gilman's edited volume *Degeneration: The Dark Side of Progress*.
82 Pick, *Faces of Degeneration*, 8.
83 Ibid., 7.
84 Nye, *Crime, Madness, and Politics*, 143.

Chapter 3

1 Balzani, "Donna crisi." For full lyrics and translation see Appendix B.
2 Ibid.
3 Ibid.
4 With the exception of Gianeri's *La donna, la moda*, scholarship on the representation of women in Italian *giornali umoristici e satirici* is almost non-existent. For information on their representation in satirical gazettes in other cultural contexts see Dolan's "The Empress's New Clothes" and Shapiro's "The Mannish New Woman." For a good overview of Italian satirical gazettes in the nineteenth and twentieth centuries, see Petrucci's *La caricatura italiana*, Gianeri's *Storia della caricatura europea*, Chiesa's *Come ridevano*, Gonnelli's *Caricatura in europa*, Lopez Nuñes's *Abbasso il fassio*, Mosca's *Antologia dell'umorismo*, and Tedesco's *La stampa satirica*.
5 I use the term "interpellation" following the work of Louis Althusser who argues, in *Lenin and Philosophy*, that one of the primary functions of ideology always is to "hail" or interpellate the subject.

6 Ellul, *Propaganda*, 75.
7 Ibid., 75. Ellul contrasts the propaganda of integration with the propaganda of agitation, or the type of heavy-handed propaganda that one normally associates with the term. Ellul describes the latter in the following manner: "In all cases, propaganda of agitation tries to stretch energies to the utmost, obtain substantial sacrifices, and induce the individual to bear heavy ordeals. It takes him out of his everyday life, his normal framework, and plunges him into enthusiasm and adventure; it opens to him hitherto unsuspected possibilities, and suggests ordinary goals that nevertheless seem to him completely within reach" (71). He also argues that "most of Hitler's propaganda was propaganda of agitation" (70). Philip Cannistraro, in his ground-breaking study of mass media in the Italian fascist period, *La fabbrica del consenso,* uses Ellul's terms in relation to the fascist context, and gives various concrete examples of how the regime used these two types of propaganda – see especially chap. 2.
8 Cannistraro, *La fabbrica del consenso,* 71. All translations of this text are mine.
9 Ibid., 72.
10 Ibid., 89.
11 Mondello, *La nuova italiana*, 111–12; translation mine.
12 Like their foreign counterparts, these gazettes most likely reached a broad audience that included men and women, older and younger people, and ranged from lower to upper class.
13 Quoted in Mintz, "The Standup Comedian," 73. This is part of a larger argument in which Douglas speaks of the joke as paradoxically both a "rite" and an "anti-rite" in her book *Implicit Meanings.* As Lawrence Mintz describes, she speaks of the joke "as public *affirmation* of shared cultural beliefs and as a *reexamination* of those beliefs" (73; emphasis added). I explore aspects of the joke as anti-rite in the last section of this chapter.
14 See Nye's book *Soft Power,* in which he describes soft power as "the ability to get what you want through attraction rather than coercion or payments" (x). My focus is particularly on the cultural aspects of soft power as illustrated, for example, in the following situations described by Nye: "Think of the impact of Franklin Roosevelt's Four Freedoms in Europe at the end of World War II; of young people behind the Iron Curtain listening to American music and news on Radio Free Europe; of Chinese students symbolizing their protests in Tiananmen Square by creating a replica of the Statue of Liberty; of newly liberated Afghans in 2001 asking for a copy of the Bill of Rights; of young Iranians today surreptitiously watching banned American videos and satellite television in the privacy of their homes. These are all examples of America's soft power" (x).

15 The cartoon should be distinguished from its popular relative, the comic strip – such as the memorable *Corriere dei Piccoli* or the ever-successful *Topolino* [Mickey Mouse] – whose serial frames show its relationship to the cinema and whose Italian name, *fumetto*, alludes to its consistent use of the speech balloon.
16 Hutcheon, *A Theory of Parody*, 16.
17 Ibid., 56. In chaps. 2 and 3 of *A Theory of Parody*, Hutcheon draws a very useful and clear distinction between parody, satire, irony, caricature, invective, burlesque, and a host of other related terms that are often confused with one another.
18 Ibid., 56; emphasis added.
19 Ibid., 79. In his article "Laughing in the Meanwhile," Samuel Weber draws attention to a similar argument about laughter when he refers to Bergson's argument that the "social function of laughter" is to enforce rules of "decorum … which must be kept in mind through repetition" (693). Weber, in turn, argues that society uses laughter to control, "through humiliation and intimidation, the transgressive tendencies of its members" (694).
20 Gianeri, *Storia della caricatura europea*, 165; emphasis added. The original reads: "La caricatura, fondamentalmente e, per natura, democratica, se caricatura autentica, ha dato un largo contributo alla Resistenza con temerari caricaturisti clandestini, polemici disegnatori di fogli sotterranei e coraggiosi combattenti" (165). The translation I give accounts for the fact that Gianeri uses the terms "satire" and "caricature" interchangeably throughout his text.
21 Ibid., 148. Luigi Tassinari presents a similar point of view in his introduction to the volume *Cento anni di satira politica in Italia*. He has this to say about satire in the fascist period: "Satire as weapon reveals all of its efficacy … Even Mussolini, personally estranged to humor, understands its pitiless efficacy, all of its political importance. Fascism, however, succeeds in silencing those who oppose it; exceptional laws condemn the pen and pencil to 'forced laziness.' Those who continue to work draw anonymous and colourless vignettes in *Il Travaso* and *Marc'Aurelio*. Only foreign newspapers and artists remain to speak of Italy and her Duce. Twenty years of silence, of abandoned debate, finally culminate in the blossoming of publications that one sees after the Liberation" (7).
22 Carabba, "Per una storia politica," 8; glosses added.
23 Ibid., 8.
24 For a good overview, see Guasta's *La Roma del Travaso*. Guasta, like Gianeri, was himself an illustrator and was for a while the director of this famous gazette.
25 For a good overview, see Chiesa's *Antologia di Marc'Aurelio*.

26 In his *Storia della caricatura europea*, Gianeri writes that Garretto "also happily took up poster design as well as refined fashion drawing. The album in which he gathered together the popular Crisis-Women, published in *Fuorisacco*, is particularly delightful" (143–4). I have been unable to locate any extant copies of *Fuorisacco* from this period, but Garretto's pamphlet can be found in the collections of the Biblioteca Nazionale Centrale in Florence.

27 For more information on the so-called *leggi fascistissime* to control the press, see Murialdi's *La stampa del regime*, Rosengarten's *The Italian Anti-fascist Press*, and Cannistraro's *La fabbrica del consenso*.

28 For more on *Il Becco giallo* see Del Buono's *Poco da Ridere*, Del Buono and Tornabuoni's *Il Becco giallo*, Chiesa's *Come ridevano*, and *Il Becco giallo: La satira di sinistra*.

29 In his famous essay "The Grey Zone," published in his last book *The Drowned and the Saved*, Levi grapples with the question of the moral accountability of certain concentration camp prisoners who, due to their unique positions, simultaneously occupied the positions of victim and perpetrator and thus could be neither condemned nor absolved.

30 For an account of censorship and the antifascist "murmurings" of *Il Travaso and Marc'Aurelio*, see Guasta and Ferri's *Jus murmurandi*.

31 See Figures 6 and 7. I discuss these cartoons in detail below.

32 This tautological relationship is not unusual in cartoons from the period, and might also serve to make the joke readable to the barely literate. On the question of reception of cartoons, Coupe notes: "It is probably true … that the lower the level of education and sophistication, the greater the impact of a picture is likely to be" ("Observations on a Theory," 83).

33 Freud, *The Joke*, 12.

34 This cartoon belongs to a series of jokes about the crisis-woman that focus on men's marital unhappiness. Another good example is Paolo Garretto's cartoon depicting a husband, a crisis-wife, and a guest at a dinner table. The crisis-wife has turned to the guest and is telling him all the foods she cannot eat: "I can't eat spaghetti, I can't eat potatoes, I can't eat meat …" [Spaghetti non ne posso mangiare, patate non ne posso mangiare, carne non ne posso mangiare ….]. The husband, sitting next to his wife, holds his head in his hands and thinks to himself "And I can't take her!" or literally "I can't *digest* her" [Ed io non la posso digerire!].

35 Eco, *A Theory of Semiotics*, 26.

36 See Crawford's *A History of the Umbrella* and Fairchilds's "The Production and Marketing of Populuxe."

37 It is worth pointing out that commodity culture, which produced the umbrella, blurred traditional roles for women and men since it involved

women in the public sphere in ways that were previously almost unimaginable. Not only did women play an important public role as consumers but, as Jacqueline Reich for one points out, they also commonly formed part of the workforce in modern urban society: "More women were employed than ever before as retail buyers, merchandising and advertising managers, personnel directors, and, of course, salesgirls and saleswomen" ("Consuming Ideologies," 202). For more on gender and commodity culture in the early twentieth century, see de Grazia's *The Sex of Things* and Mary Louise Roberts's review essay "Gender, Consumption, and Commodity Culture."

38 In addition to Irigaray's *This Sex Which Is Not One*, see Gayle Rubin's "The Traffic in Women."

39 Irigaray, *This Sex Which Is Not One*, 171.

40 Fascist labour day is also the date of the mythical founding of Rome. In *The Culture of Consent*, de Grazia mentions that this holiday was "carefully orchestrated … both because it was a fascist holiday and because in the imposing demonstrations it evoked, it was designed to eclipse altogether the memory of the May Day outing, which had been among the most cherished traditions of the socialist working class" (182). Page 204 of *The Culture of Consent* contains a photograph of the celebration.

41 The desires of the crisis-woman are shown here and elsewhere to be problematic. Luigi Bompard's cartoon "Advantages" [Vantaggi] (*Il Travaso*, October 1932) is a case in point: when one man remarks to another that since the latter's wife is gaining weight she'll "cost [him] more in basic expenses," the second man responds that "she cost [him] much more when she was on her dieting regime" [– Ma adesso che è più grassa ti costerà di più per il vitto. – Oh! Mi costava assai più quando faceva la cura per dimagrire]. This exchange suggests not only the material cost of the crisis-woman's desire to slim down (the money spent on dieting products, visits to a beauty centre for treatments, new clothing, and so on) but also the cost to the couple's sexual and interpersonal relationship. Women's desires must be controlled because they tend to excess and in doing so do not conform to the needs of the nation state. As I have shown in the previous two chapters, such desires were coded by fascism as unnatural since they did not conform to the maternal and domestic duties given to women by both "nature" and the regime.

42 See my discussion of the semiotic overlap between the modern woman and crisis-woman, and my subsequent consideration of the crisis-woman as a figure of control, in the section entitled "The Regime's Figuration of the Crisis-Woman" in chap. 1.

43 Even though there are no direct allusions to science per se in this cartoon, it is important to point out – as I argue in chap. 2 – that on the larger cultural level such normative knowledge and "truth" is undergirded by the authority of scientific discourse, and is particularly influenced by positivist scientific discourse.

44 Although this is not my project, clearly, these texts could also be read for their representations of the African and of blackness. For more on the history of fascist colonialism, see Palumbo's *A Place in the Sun*, Del Boca's *Gli italiani in Africa* and *L'Africa nella coscienza*, Ben-Ghiat and Fuller's *Italian Colonialism*, and Andall and Duncan's *Italian Colonialism*.

45 The focus on food, eating, and the thin body in these images cannot help but recall my previous mention of the privileging of the thin, saintly female body within the Catholic paradigm. The thin saintly woman, however, did not misuse her body. Instead, her restraint of appetite (both literal and metaphorical) and subsequent thinning of her body brought her closer to God.

46 Gilman, *Difference and Pathology*, 83.

47 Ibid., 85.

48 Ibid., 90.

49 See Gilman, who argues in *Difference and Pathology* that the sexualized black woman was often the "antithesis of European sexual mores" (83). He states, "It is indeed in the physical appearance of the Hottentot that the central icon for sexual difference between the European and the black was found, a deep physiological difference urged so plausibly on the basis of physical contrast that it gave pause even to early monogenetic theoreticians" (83).

50 Again see Gilman, especially his discussion of Olympia and other related visual texts in *Difference and Pathology* (81).

51 Ibid., 83.

52 De Grazia indirectly alludes to this song in *How Fascism Ruled Women* when she notes that "defying control by any single man, she [the crisis-woman] also incited male rivalries. At the close of the student dance in Padusa, Luigi Preti had his characters rush a tall, thin woman, chanting a refrain from the popular song "Donna crisi" (213).

53 Sergio Centi Sangiuliano calls Balzani "the most popular, emblematic, and representative singer-songwriter from the 1920s to the 1940s" [il cantore-autore più popolare, emblematico, rappresentivo degli Anni Venti-Quaranta] (*Balzani*, 12). Balzani notably has many songs that touch on fascist themes. One might point, for example, to "The Bachelor Tax" ["La tassa sugli scapoli"] (1928) and "Bachelors and Spinsters" ["Scapoli e

zitelle"] (1933), which both take the bachelor tax as their theme. The second argues that "zitelle," or unmarried women, should pay a tax as well because they've failed to catch the many eligible bachelors around. Also notable is the philofascist "I Wrote to the Duce" ["Ho scritto ar Duce"] (1931), in which a mother pleads the case to Mussolini that her crippled son should be let into the fascist Balilla youth group as it is his one burning desire and therefore also hers. For more on Balzani see Sangiuliano's *Balzani* as well as Martini and Tiberi's *Una vita*.

54 This parallel between lack of gastronomic and of sexual appetite can be found in the satirical cartoon as well. We have seen it obliquely suggested earlier in Onorato's "Amuleti," and it also occurs in the many cartoons that focus on marital dissatisfaction.

55 See also Cannistraro's *La fabbrica del consenso* (especially chaps. 1 and 2) for an excellent discussion of the limitations under which the Italian press was forced to work in this period.

56 For a rather scathing caricature of the effects of this punishing legislation, see the December 1925 cartoon by Guasta entitled "La libertà di stampa riceve il colpo di grazia," which was published in *Il Travaso* (reprinted in Chiesa's *Come ridevano*, 87).

57 Murialdi, *La stampa del regime*, 76.

58 Ibid., 76; emphasis added.

59 Chiesa, *Come ridevano*, 98.

60 Weber, "Laughing in the Meanwhile," 692–3.

61 "È ora di dire," *Marc'Aurelio*, 1.

62 Ibid.

63 Ibid.

64 Ibid.

65 Ibid.

66 Balazani's song also plays upon this theme, pointing out the stupidity of a man who marries a crisis-woman. He says to Nina: "And if you keep on eating breadsticks and lemons/I won't be able to marry you, I certainly don't want to come off as a dimwit!/And I don't want people to say: 'He's turned stupid!'" [E si seguiti a cibatte de grisini e de limone/io nun posso più sposatte, mica vojo fa er frescone!/E nun vojo che la gente dica: "Quello s'è scemito!"].

Chapter 4

1 See Spackman's *Fascist Virilities*.

2 De Grazia, *How Fascism Ruled Women*, 167. See also Paul Corner's article "Women in Fascist Italy" for a more specific study of women's changing

roles in working-class families of northern Italy. Corner argues that "within the social form of the worker-peasant family, fascist ideas about women found little space precisely because they were in essence opposed to the economic interests and the established economic patterns of such families" (64).

3 De Grand, "Women under Italian Fascism," 962–3.
4 Caldwell, "Reproducers of the Nation," 135.
5 Ibid., 135.
6 Passerini, *Fascism in Popular Memory,* 150.
7 Gori, *Italian Fascism,* 63.
8 For more on the reproductive fantasy, see Spackman's *Fascist Virilities;* on the fantasy of authoritarian modernization, see Ben-Ghiat's *Fascist Modernities;* and on the fantasy of society as a unified whole, see Gentile's *Il culto del littorio.*
9 Žižek, *Sublime Object,* 28.
10 Ibid., 33.
11 Ibid., 28.
12 Ibid., 32.
13 Ibid., 32.
14 Ibid., 32–3.
15 For more on chains of equivalence and their operations, see Laclau and Mouffe, *Hegemony and Socialist Strategy,* 127–9.
16 Žižek, *Sublime Object,* 126.
17 Ibid., 127.
18 Vera, "Previsioni," 24.
19 Guardi, "La crisi dell'amore," 13.
20 Ferrari, "Discursive and Ritual Sacrificial Presentation," 135.
21 Barbara Spackman's writing originally led me to think more deeply about this connection. See chap. 5 of *Fascist Virilities.*
22 Derrida, "Economies de la crise," 4.
23 For rigorous and interesting analyses of this speech, see chap. 2 of Horn's *Social Bodies,* chap. 2 of Ipsen's *Dictating Demography,* and chap. 5 of Spackman's *Fascist Virilities.*
24 Historian Lesley Caldwell explains: "The demographic initiatives of the Fascist state can be grouped under four headings: stress on the importance of marriage, incentives to produce more children and build large families, rulings on contraception and abortion and concern with infant mortality" ("Reproducers of the Nation," 116–17). Luisa Passerini gives a somewhat broader definition of the campaign. In addition to citing initiatives such as propaganda to raise the birthrate, taxes on male celibacy, and exemptions for large families, she writes that demographic policy "cannot be divorced

from the welfare and benefits provision of the regime, which was implemented through state agencies and a variety of measures. These included a very wide range of initiatives, from the Battle for Wheat to the wholesale clean-up campaign (*bonifica integrale*)" (*Fascism in Popular Memory,* 152). In this regard, she points not only to the work of the ONMI but also to "attempts to discourage urban settlement and emigration" (152).

25 Mussolini, "Il discorso dell'Ascensione," 361.
26 Ibid., 367.
27 Ibid., 362.
28 Ibid., 362–3.
29 Ibid., 361.
30 Ibid., 361.
31 Ibid., 365.
32 Ibid., 366.
33 Ibid., 364–7.
34 Ibid., 389–90.
35 According to Mitchell's *International Historical Statistics,* the population of the country at census is as follows: 1901: 32,475,000; 1911: 34,671,000; 1921: 36,406,000 (37,974,000 including Trentino Alto-Adige and Friuli Venezia-Giulia, territories acquired after World War I); 1931: 41,177,000. (6).
36 Caldwell, "Reproducers of the Nation," 127.
37 Mussolini, "Il discorso dell'Ascensione," 367.
38 Ibid., 361.
39 Ibid., 361.
40 Ibid., 390; emphasis added.
41 Ibid., 384.
42 On this project of "totalizing national transformation" as a phenomenon closely related to the project of modernization see Ben-Ghiat's *Fascist Modernities.*
43 Gentile, "La nazione," 85–86.
44 Ibid., 86.
45 Ibid., 86.
46 Mussolini, "Il discorso dell'Ascensione," 365.
47 Ibid., 382.
48 This type of demographic crisis speech is reflected in a variety of Mussolini's brief speeches or publications, such as "Demografia tedesca" ["German Demography"] (21 January 1934), "Ancora cifre" ["Statistics Again"] (25 January 1934), "Cifre" ["Statistics"] (27 February 1934), and "Regresso bianco e progresso giallo" ["White Regress and Yellow Progress"] (5 May 1934) – all of which are designed to serve as constant

reminders of the demographic crisis in both Italy and Europe and of the regime's efforts to quell that crisis.

49 Mussolini, "Il numero come forza," 214.
50 Ibid., 215.
51 Mussolini, "Il discorso dell'Ascensione," 363–4.
52 Mussolini, "Il numero come forza," 210.
53 Ibid., 210.
54 Ibid., 210.
55 Ibid., 210.
56 Ibid., 211.
57 Ibid., 212.
58 Ibid., 213.
59 Mussolini, "Discorso ai medici," 62.
60 Quine, "Racial 'Sterility' and 'Hyperfecundity,'" 98.
61 Ibid., 97.
62 Ibid., 97.
63 Mussolini, "Discorso ai medici," 60.
64 Mussolini, "Il discorso dell'Ascensione," 60.
65 Nervi, "Donna 'Crisi'," 12–13.
66 Ibid., 12.
67 Ibid., 12.

Conclusion

1 Eco, Mysterious Flame, 191.

Bibliography

Althusser, Louis. *Lenin and Philosophy and Other Essays*. Translated by Ben Brewster. New York: Monthly Review Press, 2001.

Andall, Jacqueline, and Derek Duncan, eds. *Italian Colonialism: Legacy and Memory*. Oxford: Peter Lang, 2005.

Armstrong, David. *Political Anatomy of the Body: Medical Knowledge in Britain in the Twentieth Century*. Cambridge: Cambridge University Press, 1983.

Aspesi, Natalia. *Il Lusso e l'autarchia: Storia dell'eleganza italiana 1930–1944*. Milan: Rizzoli, 1982.

Balzani, Romolo. "Donna crisi." Edizioni del TIMAClub CLAMA ML-5, compact disc, 2002. Originally released in 1933 by Odeon.

Barnes, David. *The Making of a Social Disease: Tuberculosis in Nineteenth-Century France*. Berkeley: University of California Press, 1995.

Il Becco giallo: La satira di sinistra. Milan: M&B, 2002.

Bell, Rudolph. *Holy Anorexia*. Chicago: University of Chicago Press, 1985.

Ben-Ghiat, Ruth. *Fascist Modernities: Italy 1922–1945*. Berkeley: University of California Press, 2001.

Ben-Ghiat, Ruth, and Mia Fuller, eds. *Italian Colonialism*. New York: Palgrave Macmillan, 2005.

Bossaglia, Rossana. "The Iconography of the Italian Novecento in the European Context." *Journal of Decorative and Propaganda Arts* 3 (Winter 1987): 52–65.

Brin, Irene. *Usi e costumi, 1920–1940*. Palermo: Sellerio, 1981.

Butazzi, Grazietta, ed. *1922–1943: Vent'anni di moda italiana: Proposta per un museo della moda a Milano*. Florence: Centro Di, 1980.

Butler, Judith. *Bodies That Matter: On the Discursive Limits of "Sex."* New York: Routledge, 1993.

– *Gender Trouble: Feminism and the Subversion of Identity*. New York: Routledge, 2006.

Bynum, Caroline Walker. *Holy Feast and Holy Fast: The Religious Significance of Food to Medieval Women*. Berkeley: University of California Press, 1987.

Caldwell, Lesley. "Reproducers of the Nation: Women and the Family in Fascist Policy." In *Rethinking Fascism: Capitalism, Populism, and Culture*, edited by David Forgacs, 110–141. London: Lawrence and Wishart, 1986.

Cannistraro, Philip V. *La fabbrica del consenso: Fascismo e mass media*. Rome: Laterza, 1975.

Carabba, Claudio. "Per una storia politica della satira." In *Cento anni di satira politica in Italia: 1876–1976*, edited by Enrico Gianeri and Andrea Rauch, 9–16. Florence: Guaraldi, 1976.

Chadwick, Whitney, and Tirza True Latimer. Introduction to *The Modern Woman Revisited: Paris between the Wars*, edited by Whitney Chadwick and Tirza True Latimer, xii–xxiv. New Brunswick: Rutgers University Press, 2003.

Chamberlin, J. Edward, and Sander L. Gilman, eds. *Degeneration: The Dark Side of Progress*. New York: Columbia University Press, 1985.

Chiesa, Adolfo, ed. *Antologia di Marc'Aurelio: 1931–54*. Rome: Napoleone, 1974.

– *Come ridevano gli italiani: Un viaggio nella memoria attraverso cinquant'anni di umorismo italiano*. Rome: Newton Compton, 1984.

Corner, Paul. "Women in Fascist Italy: Changing Family Roles in the Transition from an Agricultural to an Industrial Society." *European History Quarterly* 23, no. 1 (January 1993): 51–68.

Coupe, W.A. "Observations on a Theory of Political Caricature." *Comparative Studies in Society and History* 11, no. 1 (January 1969): 79–95.

Crawford, T.S. *A History of the Umbrella*. Newton Abbot: David & Charles, 1970.

De Grand, Alexander. "Women under Italian Fascism." *Historical Journal* 19, no. 4 (1976): 947–68.

de Grazia, Victoria. *The Culture of Consent: Mass Organization of Leisure in Fascist Italy*. Cambridge: Cambridge University Press, 1981.

– *How Fascism Ruled Women: Italy, 1922–1943*. Berkeley: University of California Press, 1992.

– "Nationalizing Women: The Competition between Fascist and Commercial Cultural Models in Mussolini's Italy." In *The Sex of Things: Gender and Consumption in Historical Perspective*, edited by Victoria de Grazia with Ellen Furlough, 337–58. Berkeley: University of California Press, 1996.

de Grazia, Victoria, with Ellen Furlough, eds. *The Sex of Things: Gender and Consumption in Historical Perspective*. Berkeley: University of California Press, 1996.

Del Boca, Angelo. *Gli italiani in Africa Orientale*. Bari: Laterza, 1976.

– *L'Africa nella coscienza degli Italiani: Miti, memorie, errori, sconfitte*. Rome: Laterza, 1992.

Del Buono, Oreste. *Poco da ridere: Storia privata della satira politica dall'"Asino" a "Linus."* Bari: De Donato, 1976.

Del Buono, Oreste, and Lietta Tornabuoni, eds. *Il Becco giallo: Dinamico dell'opinione pubblica, 1924–1931*. Milan: Feltrinelli, 1972.

De Longis, Rossana. "Casa e lavoro: Ruoli e modelli nelle riviste per le donne." In *La Stampa periodica romana durante il fascismo (1927–1943)*, edited by Filippo Mazzonis, 186–206. Rome: Istituto Nazionale di Studi Romani, 1998.

– "Stampa femminile." In *Dizionario del fascismo*. Vol. 2, edited by Sergio Luzzatto and Victoria de Grazia, 681–85. Turin: Einaudi, 2002–2003.

Del Principe, David. *Rebellion, Death, and Aesthetics in Italy: The Demons of Scapigliatura*. Teaneck, NJ: Farleigh Dickenson University Press, 1996.

Derrida, Jacques. "Economies de la crise." *La quinzaine littéraire* 399 (August 1983): 4–5.

Dittrich-Johansen, Helga. *Le militi dell'idea: Storia delle organizzazioni femminili del partito nazionale fascista*. Florence: L.S. Olschki, 2002.

Dolan, Therese. "The Empress's New Clothes: Fashion and Politics in Second Empire France." *Women's Art Journal* 15, no. 1 (Spring/Summer 1994): 22–8.

Douglas, Mary. *Implicit Meanings: Selected Essays in Anthropology*. London: Routledge: 1999.

– *Purity and Danger: An Analysis of Concepts of Pollution and Taboo*. Harmondsworth: Penguin, 1970.

Dowling, Linda. "The Decadent and the New Woman in the 1890s." *Nineteenth-Century Fiction* 33, no. 4 (March 1979): 434–53.

Eco, Umberto. *The Mysterious Flame of Queen Loana*. Translated by Geoffrey Brock. Orlando: Harcourt, 2006.

– *A Theory of Semiotics*. Bloomington: Indiana University Press, 1976.

Ellul, Jacques. *Propaganda: The Formation of Men's Attitudes*. New York: Alfred A. Knopf, 1965.

"È ora di dire tutto sulla donna tipo crisi!!" *Marc'Aurelio* 3, no. 21 (15 March 1933): 1.

Fairchilds, Cissie. "The Production and Marketing of Populuxe Goods in Eighteenth-Century Paris." In *Consumption and the World of Goods*, edited by John Brewer and Roy Porter, 228–48. London: Routledge, 1993.

Ferrari, Chiara. "Discursive and Ritual Sacrificial Presentation: The Rhetoric of Crisis and Resolution in Fascist Italy." *The Italianist* 23, no. 1 (June 2003): 123–49.

Fiducia (pseud.). "Aberrazioni moderne: La linea." *Maternità ed infanzia* (March 1933): 10–11.

Foucault, Michel. *The Birth of the Clinic: An Archaeology of Medical Perception.* Translated by A.M. Sheridan Smith. New York: Vintage, 1994.

– *Discipline and Punish: The Birth of the Prison.* Translated by Alan Sheridan. New York: Vintage, 1995.

– "The Eye of Power." In *Power/Knowledge: Selected Interviews and Other Writings, 1972–1977*, edited by Colin Gordon and translated by Colin Gordon, Leo Marshall, John Mepham, and Kate Soper, 146–65. New York: Pantheon, 1980.

– *The History of Sexuality.* Translated by Robert Hurley. New York: Vintage, 1988.

Freud, Sigmund. *The Joke and Its Relation to the Unconscious.* Translated by Joyce Crick. London: Penguin, 2002.

Garber, Marjorie. *Vested Interests: Cross-dressing and Cultural Anxiety.* New York: Routledge, 1997.

Gentile, Emilio. *Il culto del littorio: La sacralizzazione della politica nell'Italia fascista.* Rome: Laterza, 1993.

– "La nazione del fascismo: Alle origini del declino dello stato nazionale." In *Nazione e nazionalità in Italia*, edited by Giovanni Spadolini, 65–124. Rome: Laterza, 1994.

Gianeri, Enrico. *La donna, la moda, l'amore in tre secoli di caricatura: Con 452 stampe e caricature in nero e a colori.* Milan: Garzanti, 1942.

– *Storia della caricatura europea.* Florence: Vallecchi, 1967.

Gibson, Mary S. "Cesare Lombroso and Italian Criminology: Theory and Politics." In *Criminals and Their Scientists: The History of Criminology in International Perspective*, edited by Peter Becker and Richard F. Wetzell, 137–58. Cambridge: Cambridge University Press, 2006.

– *Prostitution and the State in Italy, 1860–1915.* New Brunswick: Rutgers University Press, 1986.

Gillette, Aaron. *Racial Theories in Fascist Italy.* London: Routledge, 2002.

Gilman, Sander. *Difference and Pathology: Stereotypes of Sexuality, Race, and Madness.* Ithaca: Cornell University Press, 1985.

– *Franz Kafka, The Jewish Patient.* New York: Routledge, 1995.

– *The Jew's Body.* New York: Routledge, 1991.

– *Picturing Health and Illness: Images of Identity and Difference.* Baltimore: Johns Hopkins University Press, 1995.

G.M. "Bellezza femminile italica." *Il giornale della donna* 15, no. 14 (July 1933): 7.

Gonnelli, Maria Pia, ed. *Caricatura in europa: Satira politica e satira borghese del secolo 19.* Florence: L. Gonnelli & Figli, 1992.

Gori, Gigliola. *Italian Fascism and the Female Body: Sport, Submissive Women and Strong Mothers.* London: Routledge, 2004.

Grillenzoni, Carlalberto. "I caratteri del fisico e del vestire considerati come fattori demografici." In *Atti del Congresso internazionale per gli studi sulla popolazione*, vol. 2, 261–69. Rome: Istituto Poligrafico dello Stato, 1933.

Gronberg, Tag. "Sonia Delaunay's Simultaneous Fashions and the Modern Woman." In *The Modern Woman Revisited: Paris between the Wars*, edited by Whitney Chadwick and Tirza True Latimer, 109–26. New Brunswick: Rutgers University Press, 2003.

Guardi, Barbara. "La crisi dell'amore." *Excelsior* 8, no. 19 (May 1932): 13.

Guasta, Guglielmo, ed. *La Roma del Travaso*. Rome: Editalia, 1973.

Guasta, Gugliemo, and Luciano Ferri. *Jus murmurandi in camicia nera*. Rome: Trevi, 1982.

Guenther, Irene. *Nazi Chic? Fashioning Women in the Third Reich*. Oxford: Berg, 2004.

Gundle, Stephen. *Bellissima: Feminine Beauty and the Idea of Italy*. New Haven: Yale University Press, 2007.

– "Feminine Beauty, National Identity and Political Conflict in Postwar Italy, 1945–54." *Contemporary European History* 8, no. 3 (1999): 359–78.

Horn, David. *The Criminal Body: Lombroso and the Anatomy of Deviance*. New York: Routledge, 2003.

– "Making Criminologists: Tools, Techniques, and the Production of Scientific Authority." In *Criminals and Their Scientists: The History of Criminology in International Perspective*, edited by Peter Becker and Richard F. Wetzell, 317–36. Cambridge: Cambridge University Press, 2006.

– *Social Bodies: Science, Reproduction, and Italian Modernity*. Princeton: Princeton University Press, 1994.

Hutcheon, Linda. *A Theory of Parody: The Teachings of Twentieth-Century Art Forms*. New York: Methuen, 1985.

Ipsen, Carl. *Dictating Demography: The Problem of Population in Fascist Italy*. Cambridge: Cambridge University Press, 1996.

– "Pende, Nicola." In *Dizionario del fascismo*. Vol. 2, edited by Victoria de Grazia and Sergio Luzzatto, 357–9. Turin: Einaudi, 2003.

Irigaray, Luce. *This Sex Which Is Not One*. Translated by Catherine Porter with Carolyn Burke. Ithaca: Cornell University Press, 1985.

Kraus, Elizabeth. "Forward vs. Reverse Gear: Politics of Proliferation and Resistance in the Italian Fascist State." *Journal of Historical Sociology* 7, no. 3 (September 1994): 261–88.

Laclau, Ernesto, and Chantal Mouffe. *Hegemony and Socialist Strategy: Towards a Radical Democratic Politics*. London: Verso, 1985.

Laver, James. *Women's Dress in the Jazz Age*. London: Hamish Hamilton, 1964.

Lawlor, Clark. *Consumption and Literature: The Making of the Romantic Disease.* Houndmills, UK: Palgrave MacMillan, 2007.

Levi, Primo. *The Drowned and the Saved.* Translated by Raymond Rosenthal. New York: Vintage, 1989.

Livi-Bacci, Massimo. *A History of Italian Fertility during the Last Two Centuries.* Princeton: Princeton University Press, 1977.

Lombroso, Cesare. *Criminal Man.* Edited by Mary Gibson and Nicole Hahn Rafter. Translated by Mary Gibson, Nicole Hahn Rafter, and Mark Seymour. Durham: Duke University Press, 2006.

– *La donna delinquente, la prostituta e la donna normale.* Turin: Fratelli Bocca, 1927.

– *L'uomo delinquente in rapporto all'antropologia, alla giurisprudenza ed alle discipline carcerarie.* Turin: Fratelli Bocca, 1924.

Lombroso, Cesare, and Guglielmo Ferrero. *Criminal Woman, the Prostitute, and the Normal Woman.* Edited and translated by Nicole Hahn Rafter and Mary Gibson. Durham: Duke University Press, 2004.

Lopez Nuñes, Sergio. *Abbasso il fassio: La satira politica nel Ventennio.* Milan: Baldini & Castoldi, 1999.

Mag (pseud.)."Primi tepori estivi, primi abiti leggeri." *Lidel* (May 1925): 33–6.

Martini, Luigi, and Maurizio Tiberi. *Una vita per la canzone: Romolo Balzani.* Castelnuovo di Porto: Edizioni TIMAClub, 2002.

McRobbie, Angela. "Bridging the Gap: Feminism, Fashion and Consumption." *Feminist Review* 55 (Spring 1997): 73–89.

Meldini, Piero. *Sposa e madre esemplare: Ideologia e politica della donna e della famiglia durante il fascismo.* Rimini: Guaraldi, 1975.

Mintz, Lawrence. "The Standup Comedian as Social and Cultural Mediator." *American Quarterly* 37, no. 1 (Spring 1985): 71–80.

Mitchell, Brian R. *International Historical Statistics, Europe, 1750–1988.* Basingstoke, UK: Macmillan, 1992.

Mondello, Elisabetta. *La nuova italiana: La donna nella stampa e nella cultura del ventennio.* Turin: Riuniti, 1987.

Mosca, Giovanni, ed. *Antologia dell'umorismo: Umoristi italiani 1890–1925.* Rome: Editalia, 1972.

Murialdi, Paolo. *La stampa del regime fascista.* Rome: Laterza, 1986.

Mussolini, Benito. "Discorso ai Medici." In *Opera Omnia.* Vol. 25, edited by Edoardo and Duilio Susmel, 58–62. Florence: La Fenice, 1951.

– "Il discorso dell'Ascensione." In *Opera Omnia.* Vol. 27, edited by Edoardo and Duilio Susmel, 350–390. Florence: La Fenice, 1951.

– "Il numero come forza." In *Opera Omnia.* Vol. 23, edited by Edoardo and Duilio Susmel, 209–16. Florence: La Fenice, 1951.

Nervi, Camilla. "Donna 'Crisi.'" *Maternità ed infanzia* 8, no. 2 (February 1934): 12–13.

Nye, Joseph. *Soft Power: The Means to Success in World Politics*. New York: PublicAffairs, 2004.

Nye, Robert A. *Crime, Madness, and Politics: The Medical Concept of National Decline*. Princeton: Princeton University Press, 1984.

Offen, Karen. *European Feminisms 1700–1950: A Political History*. Stanford: Stanford University Press, 2000.

Osborne, Thomas. "On Anti-Medicine and Clinical Reason." In *Reassessing Foucault: Power, Medicine and the Body*, edited by Colin Jones and Roy Porter, 28–47. London: Routledge, 1994.

Ott, Katherine. *Fevered Lives: Tuberculosis in American Culture Since 1870*. Cambridge: Harvard University Press, 1996.

Palumbo, Patrizia. *A Place in the Sun: Italian Colonial Culture from Post-Unification to the Present*. Berkeley: University of California Press, 2003.

Passerini, Luisa. *Fascism in Popular Memory: The Cultural Experience of the Turin Working Class*. Translated by Robert Lumley and Jude Bloomfield. Cambridge: Cambridge University Press, 1987.

Paulicelli, Eugenia. *Fashion under Fascism: Beyond the Blackshirt*. Oxford: Berg, 2004.

Pende, Nicola. *Bonifica umana razionale e biologia politica*. Bologna: Cappelli editore, 1933.

– "Costituzione e fecondità." In *Atti del Congresso internazionale per gli studi sulla popolazione*, vol. 3, 77–102. Rome: Istituto Poligrafico dello Stato, 1933.

– "Maternità, estetica e salute femminile." *Maternità ed Infanzia*. (December, 1934): 8.

– *Trattato di biotipologia umana individuale e sociale*. Milan: Casa Editrice Dottor Francesco Vallardi, 1939.

Petrucci, Carlo Alberto. *La caricatura italiana dell'ottocento*. Rome: De Luca, 1954.

Piccoli, Valentino. "Le grasse e le magre." *Amica* 4, no. 11 (November 1932): 4–5.

Pick, Daniel. *Faces of Degeneration: A European Disorder, c. 1848–1918*. Cambridge: Cambridge University Press, 1993.

Pickering-Iazzi, Robin. *Mothers of Invention: Women, Fascism and Italian Culture*. Minneapolis: University of Minnesota Press, 1995.

Quine, Maria S. "Racial 'Sterility' and 'Hyperfecundity' in Fascist Italy: Biological Politics of Sex and Reproduction." *Fascism* 1 (2012): 92–144.

Reich, Jacqueline. "Consuming Ideologies: Fascism, Commodification, and Female Subjectivity in Mario Camerini's *Grandi Magazzini*." *Annali d'Italianistica* 16 (1998): 195–212.

Riviere, Joan. "Womanliness as a Masquerade." In *Formations of Fantasy*, edited by Victor Burgin, James Donald, and Cora Kaplan, 38–44. London: Methuen, 1986.

Roberts, Mary Louise. *Civilization without Sexes: Reconstructing Gender in Postwar France, 1917–1927*. Chicago: University of Chicago Press, 1994.

– "Gender, Consumption, and Commodity Culture." *The American Historical Review* 103, no. 3 (June 1998): 817–44.

– "Samson and Delilah Revisited: The Politics of Fashion in 1920s France." In *The Modern Woman Revisited: Paris between the Wars*, edited by Whitney Chadwick and Tirza True Latimer, 64–94. New Brunswick: Rutgers University Press, 2003.

Ronchi, Stellina. "La moda italiana." *Il giornale della donna* 15, no. 10 (May 1933): 4.

Rose, Nikolas. "Medicine, History and the Present." In *Reassessing Foucault: Power, Medicine and the Body*, edited by Colin Jones and Ray Porter, 48–72. New York: Routledge, 1994.

Rosengarten, Frank. *The Italian Anti-fascist Press (1919–1945): From the Legal Opposition Press to the Underground Newspapers of World War II*. Cleveland: University of Case Western Reserve Press, 1968.

Rubin, Gayle. "The Traffic in Women: Notes on the 'Political Economy' of Sex." In *Toward an Anthropology of Women*, edited by Rayna Reiter, 157–210. New York: Monthly Review Press, 1975.

Sangiuliano, Sergio Centi. *Balzani: Fra spettacolo e folklore*. Rome: Nuova Editrice Spada, 1986.

Shapiro, Susan C. "The Mannish New Woman: *Punch* and Its Precursors." *Review of English Studies* 42, no. 168 (November 1991): 510–22.

Spackman, Barbara. *Fascist Virilities: Rhetoric, Ideology and Social Fantasy in Italy*. Minneapolis: University of Minnesota Press, 1996.

Steele, Valerie. *Fashion and Eroticism: Ideals of Feminine Beauty from the Victorian Era to the Jazz Age*. Oxford: Oxford University Press, 1985.

Tassinari, Luigi. Introduction to *Cento anni di satira politica in Italia: 1876–1976*, edited by Enrico Gianeri and Andrea Rauch, 6–7. Florence: Guaraldi, 1976.

Tedesco, Viva. *La stampa satirica in Italia: 1860–1914*. Milan: Angeli, 1991.

Toniolo, Gianni. *L'economia dell'Italia fascista*. Rome: Laterza, 1980.

Tranfaglia, Nicola. *La stampa del regime, 1932–1943: Le veline del Minculpop per orientare l'informazione*. Milan: Bompiani, 2005.

Ulrichs, Karl Heinrich. *The Riddle of "Man-Manly" Love: The Pioneering Work on Male Homosexuality*. Translated by Michael A. Lombardi-Nash. Buffalo: Prometheus, 1994.

Vera (pseud.). "La moda: Commenti e consigli." *Lidel* 14, no. 6 (June 1932): 22–7.

– "Previsioni." *Lidel* 12, no. 9 (September 1931): 24–33.

Veronesi, Giulia. *Into the Twenties: Style and Design 1909–1929.* Translated by Diana Barran. London: Thames and Hudson, 1968.
Weber, Samuel. "Laughing in the Meanwhile." *MLN* 102, no. 4 (September 1987): 691–706.
Wilson, Elizabeth. *Adorned in Dreams: Fashion and Modernity*. Berkeley: University of California Press, 1985.
Žižek, Slavoj. *The Sublime Object of Ideology*. London: Verso Books, 1989.

Index

www.ingramcontent.com/pod-product-compliance
Lightning Source LLC
Chambersburg PA
CBHW020324270725
30045CB00009B/50/J

* 9 7 8 1 4 4 2 6 4 9 6 7 5 *